BESH BIG EASY

101 Home Cooked New Orleans Recipes

JOHN BESH

PRODUCED BY DOROTHY KALINS INK

PHOTOGRAPHS BY MAURA MCEVOY

DESIGN BY DON MORRIS DESIGN

Other Books by John Besh

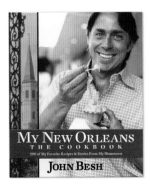

MY NEW ORLEANS, The Cookbook
200 of My Favorite Recipes & Stories from My Hometown

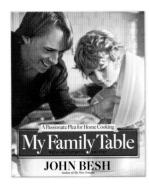

MY FAMILY TABLE
A Passionate Plea for Home Cooking

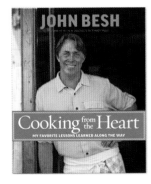

COOKING FROM THE HEART
My Favorite Lessons Learned Along the Way

❝ This is not cheffy food, this is just go-o-o-d home cooking. ❞

INTRODUCTION

Why am I writing **Besh Big Easy** when so many great books about my hometown, including my very own **My New Orleans,** have already been written? For starters, I'm typing these words from my writer's nook overlooking the very bayou that I grew up on; in the deep shadows of live oak trees hung with Spanish moss, and among the towering cypress trees we played in as children. I've evolved much since those days and, for that matter, my cooking has evolved, too.

I wrote my first book, **My New Orleans,** in the horrific wake of the disastrous Hurricane Katrina, with great passion for preserving our beautiful culture—a culture I believed was threatened. My children were younger then, and my cooking at home was relegated to extravagant Sunday suppers, holidays, and other family gatherings.

I cooked at home like a chef, often bringing in hard-to-find ingredients from my restaurants, cooking delicious renditions of the traditional dishes of New Orleans, but with a deliberate, chef's spin on them. Today, I cook more like a scruffy, grizzly, bearded dad. I worry less over the particular town the sausage is made in, and care more about the soul of each dish I want to feed to those I love most. I don't destroy the kitchen any longer when I cook; I cook on a simpler level, using as few ingredients, pots, and pans as possible.

My children are older and I'm a bit wiser about cherishing the remaining time they have living on this very bayou that has had such an impact on me.

The argument could be made that today I cook more like my mother and grandmother than ever. I cherish the gift of culture that my family enjoys at our family table, and I hope that you at home will enjoy these authentic flavors through the delicious, simple recipes in this book.

Besh Big Easy is a deliberate paperback. I don't want it sitting on your coffee table, I want it well-used in your kitchen. I hope notes are made, photographs are splattered, and pages are frayed from constant use. I want you to cook, love, and share the recipes on these pages without worrying about finding the right ingredients or mastering complicated culinary processes. It's my goal to encourage you to cook and break bread with friends, family, even strangers. I truly believe that if we do this, the world will be a better place!

MY BIG EASY INGREDIENTS

" I don't want the lack of a specific ingredient to keep you from cooking. It's important for me to communicate an understanding of how these recipes are done, and once you get that spirit, well, in most cases, use whatever you can get your hands on. "

Holy Trinity: The holy trinity of New Orleans cooking is onion, celery, bell pepper. But it can be overplayed. We always have onions and celery in the house, but we don't worry if there's no bell pepper.

My *Besh Big Easy* Holy Trinity: Tabasco (Tabasco.com), Zatarain's Shrimp & Crab Boil (zatarains.com), and Italian bread crumbs. With Worcestershire a distant fourth. About those bread crumbs: You can say all you want about making your own, but look in the cupboard of any New Orleans cook and you will find that box of seasoned bread crumbs!

Tomatoes: Unless your fresh tomatoes are ripe to bursting, don't even bother. Use good canned tomatoes instead. In season, make yourself some Cherry Tomato Five-Minute Sauce (page 84) and freeze it.

Stock: Sure, making your own stock delivers the most flavor: see my Go-To Chicken Stock (page 27). I use the same principle for fish, shellfish, shrimp, and crab stocks, too (see the Variations). Yes, of course you can use prepared broth. But

in a pinch, I use what so many New Orleans home cooks use: water.

Mayonnaise: All these recipes use mayo from a jar—that's easy! I love our local brand, Blue Plate; it's what I grew up on.

Olive oil: When I ask for olive oil, I like extra-virgin, because it filters out impurities. It's the only olive oil I ever use.

Mustard: I love our grainy, vinegary Creole mustard, but if you can't find it, use any good sharp, whole grain mustard.

Green onions: In New Orleans, we call them green onions. To you they may be scallions— same thing! But you don't just add green onions for color. They taste great, too. Thyme and green onions—these are the flavors I grew up with.

Oysters: I love our plump, juicy Louisiana oysters, so use the biggest, freshest local oysters you can find.

Crab: We're lucky in New Orleans, we get the freshest jumbo lump blue crabmeat from the crabs in Lake Pontchartrain. I know

Rice: I cook with long-grain Louisiana white rice (that *is* chauvinism), but for these recipes, everyday white rice is just fine. See my Big Easy way to cook rice (page 116).

Cheese: I use our local farmer cheese, Creole cream cheese, when I can; but it's fine to use sour cream, crème fraîche, or Greek yogurt instead.

good-quality crab meat is harder to come by in the rest of the country. Always use the best you can find, and make sure to pick through for any bits of shell. When a recipe calls for whole crabs, I mean the largest blue crabs you can find.

Crawfish: Wild crawfish are in season from mid-winter until about May. Order whole crawfish in season from Kenney's Seafood, in Slidell, LA, 985-643-2717. Order cultivated crawfish year-round from lacrawfish.com.

Shrimp: Wild American shrimp are now widely available; it's the only shrimp I want you to cook with. And that's not just drum-beating for my state. Imported shrimp are raised with dubious health standards, both in their breeding ponds and the well-being of their workers. Unlike other shellfish, shrimp freezes well, so it's okay to buy frozen.

Crab boil seasoning: I like Zatarain's liquid concentrated or powdered Shrimp & Crab Boil seasoning. If you can't find it, use another shellfish boil mixture or dip into My Creole Spice Jar (right).

Sausage: I grew up on the German-inspired smoked sausages and andouille from Jacob's (cajunsausage.com) and Bailey's (baileysandouille.com) in Louisiana's sausage-making capital, LaPlace, just west of New Orleans. But any good smoked pork, beef, or even chicken sausage is great. When I call for fresh pork sausage, I mean sausage that has not been smoked. I use it out of the casing and crumbled.

My Creole Spice Jar: I promised not to get too fussy with ingredients in this book, but in my heart of hearts, I really believe you need this simple spice mix to infuse your cooking with authentic flavor.

2 tablespoons celery salt	1 tablespoon garlic powder
1 tablespoon sweet paprika	1 tablespoon onion powder
1 tablespoon coarse sea salt	2 teaspoons cayenne pepper
1 tablespoon black pepper	½ teaspoon ground allspice.

Mix it together in a small jar, shake it up well, and use it to season your gumbos (and soups and stews). It'll last for months.

MUFFULETTA

CONSISTS OF

Imported Salami, Ham & Cheese,
Mortadella
"Our Special Olive Salad"
on Italian Bread

Chapter
1
EASY
APPS

> ❝ I come from people who have serious pride in their Southern hospitality. Any meal is an excuse for a party. While American foodways have become alarmingly homogenized, our cooking in New Orleans is still vibrantly alive. We aren't the most progressive group, but we do have values. We value time and waste as much of it as we can. ❞

ff Spending time in France just made me love our New Orleans way with classic preparations even more. *Ravigoter* means to refresh, and that's just what this sauce does to crabmeat (or shrimp). It is perked up with a touch of vinegar and bright lemon juice. We don't want it to be too spicy, but we want it to have some life. The rich and briny sauce holds together succulent lumps of jumbo blue crab. But I'll make the tangy sauce to serve with roast beef, too. **JJ**

Crabmeat Ravigote

✦ Serves 6-8

¾ cup mayonnaise
2 heaping tablespoons prepared horseradish
2 teaspoons Dijon mustard
2 green onions, chopped
1 teaspoon rice wine vinegar

Big pinch cayenne pepper
Juice of 1 lemon
1 pound crabmeat
1½ teaspoons salt
Tabasco

Combine all ingredients in a mixing bowl except the crabmeat, salt, and Tabasco. Whisk until smooth. Gently fold in the crabmeat, then add the salt and a dash of Tabasco.

Crabmeat Spinach Dip

> 🏠🏠 This easy and delicious green dip has a base of Crabmeat Ravigote. I like to serve it surrounded by lots of cut up fresh vegetables. 🏠🏠

✦ Serves 6-8

1 tablespoon olive oil
1 clove garlic, thinly sliced
½ teaspoon crushed red pepper flakes
1 pound fresh spinach or kale, finely chopped

8 ounces cream cheese, sour cream, or Greek yogurt
Crabmeat Ravigote

Heat the oil in a large skillet, then add the garlic and pepper flakes. Cook for a moment then add the spinach. Stir well for 2 minutes and remove from the heat.

Transfer the spinach to a small bowl, stir in the cream cheese until well combined, then fold in the crabmeat ravigote.

Walter is a retired ship captain buddy who lives down the bayou. I love his pickled crabs and finally persuaded him to give me the recipe. He pickles the crabs for 24 hours, a method he says is traditional, but he's the only guy I've ever seen do it that way.

Walter's Pickled Crabs

✦ Serves 4-6

6	tablespoons lemon or lime juice	2	cloves garlic, thinly sliced
6	tablespoons vinegar	1	serrano or other hot chile, thinly sliced
2	tablespoons Creole mustard	12	boiled or steamed crabs, quartered
6	tablespoons sugar	3	green onions, chopped
	Salt and pepper		

Bring 1 cup water to a boil in a small saucepan. Add the lemon juice, vinegar, mustard, sugar, salt, pepper, garlic, and chile and stir until the sugar dissolves.

Put the crabs in a large bowl, pour in the warm mixture, and toss well. Add the green onions and refrigerate at least a couple of hours before serving, as pictured above.

If you're wondering what to do with all the crab claws left from making a recipe like Mr. Sam's Stuffed Crabs (page 110), here's the perfect way to use them.

Garlicky Baked Crab Claws

✦ Serves 6

¼ cup olive oil
3 onions, chopped
3 cloves garlic, sliced
Pinch crushed red pepper flakes

Pinch herbes de Provence
¼ cup dry vermouth
8 tablespoons butter, cubed
1 pound crab claws

Preheat the oven to 400°. Heat the oil in a small saucepan over medium heat. Add the onions, garlic, pepper flakes, herbs, and vermouth and cook until the liquid is reduced by half. Whisk the butter into the vermouth reduction.

Place the crab claws in a baking dish and pour the sauce over them. Bake about 5 minutes or until the crab claws are heated through.

❝ This dish is pure comfort food. I love to make the white sauce in the pan, then add the crab and really fresh cheese, like the Italian white melting cheeses— fontina, mozzarella, or provolone. Sherry adds sweetness to all that cheesy, crabby goodness. **❞**

Crabmeat au Gratin

✦ Serves 4-6

4 tablespoons butter	4 dashes Tabasco
2 green onions, chopped	Salt and pepper
1 clove garlic, minced	1 pound crabmeat
4 tablespoons flour	1½ cups grated mozzarella cheese
1½ cups milk	½ cup grated cheddar cheese
2 tablespoons sherry	
2 dashes Zatarain's Shrimp & Crab Boil	

Preheat the oven to 400°. Melt the butter in a heavy skillet, add the green onions and garlic, and soften over medium-high heat, stirring often. Add the flour and continue stirring for about 5 minutes, then add the milk and keep stirring until the sauce thickens, about another 5 minutes. Add the sherry, crab boil seasoning, Tabasco, salt, and pepper and remove from heat.

Combine the mozzarella and cheddar. Mix the crabmeat and 1¾ cups of the cheeses into the skillet. Pour into a baking dish and top with remaining cheese. Bake for about 10 minutes, until golden brown and bubbly. Serve with plenty of bread for scooping.

❝ These mushrooms are almost hearty enough to be a meal in themselves. Sometimes I'll make the stuffing a day ahead, stuff the caps, and refrigerate them on a baking sheet. A half hour before serving, I'll pop them in the oven till they're brown and crisp. **❞**

Shrimp & Crawfish Stuffed Mushrooms

✦ Serves 8

- 3 tablespoons butter
- 16 large button mushrooms, stems reserved and diced
- 2 green onions, chopped
- 1 stalk celery, chopped
- 2 cloves garlic, minced
- ½ pound medium wild American shrimp, peeled, deveined, and chopped
- ½ pound shelled crawfish tails, chopped
- ½ cup Italian dried bread crumbs
- Salt and pepper
- Olive oil
- ¼ cup grated Parmesan cheese

Preheat the oven to 375°. In a large skillet over medium heat, combine the butter, chopped mushroom stems, green onions, celery, and garlic. Cook until the vegetables have softened, about 5 minutes. Add the shrimp and crawfish and cook another 3 minutes. Add the bread crumbs, salt, and pepper. Remove from the heat and let the stuffing cool.

Spoon a generous dollop of the stuffing into each mushroom cap and place on a baking sheet. Drizzle a bit of olive oil over the tops and sprinkle with the Parmesan. Bake for 15–20 minutes until the tops are golden brown.

Oysters Stuffed with Shrimp & Crab

✦ Makes 2 dozen

½ pound medium wild American shrimp, peeled, deveined, and chopped	Pinch crushed red pepper flakes
4 tablespoons butter	½ recipe Crabmeat Ravigote (page 2)
2 green onions, chopped	2 dozen oysters on the half shell
¼ cup grated Parmesan cheese	1 lemon, halved
½ cup Italian dried bread crumbs	Tabasco

Preheat the broiler. Cook the shrimp with the butter in a skillet over medium-high heat for about 3 minutes, just so they're about half-cooked. Transfer to a mixing bowl and combine with the green onions, Parmesan, bread crumbs, and pepper flakes. Mix in the crabmeat ravigote.

To steady the oysters, crumple aluminum foil on a baking sheet and settle in the oysters. Spoon crab and shrimp stuffing onto each shell. Broil about a minute, until the stuffing is golden brown. Serve with a squeeze of lemon juice and a dash of Tabasco.

These lightly fried fritters of crawfish (or shrimp or crab) are irresistible. I like to make a batch for my friends to devour while they're hanging out in the kitchen, waiting for me to finish cooking dinner. I make the Tabasco Cream Sauce ahead and encourage dipping.

Crawfish Beignets with Tabasco Cream Sauce

✦ Serves 6-8

Canola oil
½ pound shelled crawfish tails, chopped
1½ teaspoons celery salt
Pinch garlic powder
Pinch cayenne pepper
¼ teaspoon salt
Pinch black pepper

2 green onions, chopped
2 eggs, beaten
½ cup milk
1¼ cups flour
1½ teaspoons baking powder
Tabasco Cream Sauce

In a small saucepan, heat at least 3 inches of canola oil to 350°. Season the crawfish with the celery salt, garlic powder, cayenne, salt, and black pepper in a large mixing bowl. Add the green onions, eggs, milk, flour, and baking powder and mix just until a batter forms.

Working in batches, carefully spoon heaping tablespoons of beignet batter into the oil. Turn the beignets every few minutes with a slotted spoon. Fry until golden brown. Remove from the oil and drain on paper towels. Serve immediately with the Tabasco cream sauce.

TABASCO CREAM SAUCE

✦ Makes about 1 cup

¾ cup mayonnaise
2 cloves garlic, peeled
2 green onions, chopped
6 cherry tomatoes
1 tablespoon Tabasco
1 tablespoon green Tabasco
Pinch salt

Combine all ingredients in a blender and puree until smooth.

" Our Louisiana oysters are so big and plump and juicy, they don't need much. Just do it up old school with my favorite sauces: Cocktail, Mignonette, and good old horseradish. **"**

Oysters with Cocktail & Mignonette Sauces

COCKTAIL SAUCE

✦ Makes about 1 cup

In a small bowl, mix together ¾ cup ketchup, 2 tablespoons prepared horseradish, 2 tablespoons fresh lemon juice, a pinch of salt, and a dash of Tabasco. Serve with raw oysters.

MIGNONETTE SAUCE

✦ Makes ½ cup

In a small bowl, whisk together 1 small finely diced shallot, ½ cup red wine vinegar, 1 teaspoon ground black pepper, and a big pinch sea salt. Serve with raw oysters.

Grilled Oysters with Herb Garlic Butter

✦ Makes 2 dozen

HERB GARLIC BUTTER

½ pound butter, at room temperature	1 green onion, chopped
1 teaspoon lemon juice	1 clove garlic, minced
1 tablespoon chopped fresh parsley leaves	1 teaspoon crushed red pepper flakes
1 teaspoon minced fresh tarragon	2 dozen oysters on the half shell

Make the herb garlic butter: Combine the butter, lemon juice, parsley, tarragon, green onion, garlic, and pepper flakes in a blender and process until well combined. Wrap the butter in plastic wrap and roll it into a tight cylinder; chill until firm, at least an hour.

Preheat the grill. Slice a piece of herb butter over each oyster and place on the grill. Cook the oysters until the butter melts and the oysters start to curl and bubble around the edges.

❛❛ Oysters on the grill are irresistible appetizers for a backyard celebration. Folks just can't wait to get their hands on them. The herb garlic butter has so many other good uses: spoon it on pasta, throw it in a pan and sauté shrimp in it, or just spread it on toast. Make the butter ahead so it solidifies. ❜❜

❝ This is a perfect way to enjoy our plump Louisiana oysters at the table, cloaked in my go-to topping: a crispy mix of bread crumbs, Parmesan cheese, and lots of olive oil. I usually make this gratin in a big ovenproof dish. But I also love it when everyone has an individual golden brown ramekin straight from the oven. ❞

Oyster Gratin with Horseradish & Parmesan

✦ Serves 6-8

- 4 tablespoons butter
- ¼ cup flour
- ½ onion, chopped
- 2 cloves garlic, thinly sliced
- 2 cups milk
- 2 heaping tablespoons prepared horseradish
- Salt and pepper
- 3 dozen oysters, shucked, drained, and patted dry
- ⅓ cup dried bread crumbs
- ⅓ cup grated Parmesan cheese
- ⅓ cup olive oil
- 1 teaspoon crushed red pepper flakes

Melt the butter in a large saucepan over medium heat, whisk in the flour, and whip up a roux, whisking until it turns blond, about 5 minutes. Add the onions and garlic, lower the heat, and continue cooking and stirring until the onions are soft.

Slowly whisk in the milk, bring to a boil, then immediately reduce the heat to low. Let the sauce simmer, stirring occasionally, until it's thick enough to coat the back of a spoon, about 30 minutes. Remove the pan from the heat and stir in the horseradish, salt, and pepper. Cover the saucepan with plastic wrap and let cool.

Preheat the oven to 450°. Salt and pepper the oysters and place them in a baking dish in a single layer. Pour the cooled sauce evenly over the oysters.

In another bowl, mix the bread crumbs, Parmesan, olive oil, and pepper flakes until the oil moistens the bread crumbs. Sprinkle over the oysters and sauce in the baking dish. Bake for about 15 minutes or until the topping turns golden brown.

❝ Who doesn't love fried oysters? Most places around New Orleans just roll the raw oysters in bread crumbs and seasonings, but I think one more step makes a big difference in lightness: I whip a few egg whites into a foam and dip in the oysters before they hit the batter. I make my ranch dressing with paddlefish roe. You can make the dressing long before you fry your oysters. ❞

Crispy Fried Oysters with Caviar Ranch Dressing

✦ Makes 3 dozen

3 cups flour	4 egg whites, beaten
1 cup cornmeal	Canola oil
1 cup dried bread crumbs	Salt
2 tablespoons from My Creole Spice Jar (page xi)	1 recipe Caviar Ranch Dressing
3 dozen oysters, shucked, drained, and patted dry	

Combine the flour, cornmeal, bread crumbs, and Creole Spices in a medium bowl.

In another bowl, toss the oysters with the beaten egg whites. When you're ready to batter and fry them, remove the oysters from the egg whites and toss them into the seasoned flour mix.

Heat at least 3 inches of canola oil to 350° in a small saucepan. Fry a few oysters at a time, turning with a slotted spoon for several minutes, until golden brown. Drain on paper towels and salt well.

When all the oysters are fried, serve them up with the dressing on the side.

CAVIAR RANCH DRESSING

✦ Makes about ½ cup

¼ cup buttermilk	¼ teaspoon celery salt
¼ cup mayonnaise	Dash Tabasco
1 tablespoon sour cream	1 tablespoon paddlefish roe
1 teaspoon lemon juice	2 teaspoons chopped chives
1 shallot, minced	Salt and pepper
1 clove garlic, minced	

In a food processor, blend together the buttermilk, mayonnaise, sour cream, lemon juice, shallot, garlic, celery salt, and Tabasco. Transfer to a bowl and add the paddlefish roe, chives, and salt and pepper as needed. Chill until ready to use.

Bam Bam Shrimp

✦ Serves 4

 These are the potato chips of the shrimp world: crispy fried shrimp tossed with a chili mayonnaise. I dare you to eat just one. 🔖🔖

Canola oil
1 cup cornstarch
1 cup rice flour
2½ cups soda water
½ pound medium wild American shrimp, peeled and deveined
   Salt
2 tablespoons sambal chili paste
½ cup mayonnaise

Heat 3 inches of oil in a small saucepan to 350°. In a mixing bowl, combine the cornstarch, rice flour, and soda water. Dip the shrimp into the batter and drip off excess. Fry the shrimp until crispy. Drain on paper towels and salt well.

In a large bowl, whisk together the chili paste and mayonnaise. Add the hot fried shrimp, toss, and serve.

Shrimp Remoulade

✦ Serves 12

- 1 cup mayonnaise
- ¼ cup Dijon mustard
- 2 tablespoons prepared horseradish
- 2 green onions, chopped
- ½ stalk celery, minced
- 2 tablespoons chopped fresh parsley
- 1 clove garlic, minced
- 1 tablespoon white wine vinegar

- Juice of 1 lemon
- 1 teaspoon Tabasco
- ¼ teaspoon cayenne pepper
- Salt

- 24 jumbo wild American shrimp or 3 dozen smaller shrimp, boiled in spicy water (see note, right), drained, and peeled

For the remoulade, combine all ingredients but the shrimp in a medium bowl and mix well.

At least 2 hours before serving, stir the cooked shrimp into the remoulade sauce and marinate.

❝ I serve this scrumptiously sauced shrimp in a hospitable leaf of Bibb lettuce as a lovely, old-fashioned first course at Sunday dinner. Here's the way to get the most intense shrimp flavor: Boil the shrimp for 3 to 5 minutes in a pot of spicy, salty, lemony water spiked with onion, garlic, paprika, cayenne, whole coriander seeds, and a couple of bay leaves. ❞

In New Orleans, we make Stuffed Artichokes as an offering of abundance at St. Joseph's Day feasts. They're sold, stuffed and ready to go, at many little food shops around town. We consider them 'social food': a dish you'd put in the middle of the table. Just one look at these abundant artichokes and you know: This is some good!

Stuffed Artichokes

✦ Serves 6

3 large or 6 small artichokes
3 cloves garlic, thinly sliced
1¼ cups olive oil
1 teaspoon crushed red pepper flakes
2 cups dried bread crumbs
1 cup grated Parmesan cheese
1 sprig fresh basil, chopped
Salt and pepper

1 pound medium wild American shrimp, peeled, deveined, and chopped
1 pound crabmeat
2 green onions, chopped
Pinch herbes de Provence

Preheat the oven to 350°. Cut the stems off the artichokes, peel away the bottom leaves, and trim the spines off the remaining leaves. Simmer the artichokes in a big pot of salted water for about 20 minutes. Remove and drain upside down on paper towels.

Make the stuffing by sweating the garlic in 1 cup of the olive oil in a large skillet over medium heat. Add the pepper flakes and bread crumbs and cook 3 minutes to toast the crumbs. Transfer to a large bowl and fold in the Parmesan and basil.

Salt and pepper the shrimp and sauté in 2 tablespoons of the olive oil for 2 minutes, then add the crabmeat, green onions, and herbes de Provence. Add the bread crumb mixture and stir to combine. Spoon stuffing in between the leaves of the artichokes, the more the better!

Once the artichokes are stuffed, drizzle the remaining 2 tablespoons oil over the tops. Place the artichokes in a baking dish and cover with aluminum foil. Bake for 35 minutes. Remove the foil and bake for an additional 10–15 minutes or until the stuffing is golden brown.

Our wives are never sure whether we go to the hunting camp to hunt, or to cook, or just to hang out together. But you'd better believe we do all of those things obsessively and competitively and have done so with the same group since we were all a whole lot younger: Drew Mire, Blake LeMaire, and my brother-in-law, Patrick Berrigan, the selfsame Patty Joe of this infamously tasty recipe. It's even better if you've shot the ducks.

Patty Joe's Duck Poppers

✦ Makes 16

1½ pounds duck breasts, skin removed and cut into 16 strips, about ¼ inch thick and 2 inches wide

Salt and pepper

1 tablespoon chopped fresh thyme

1 tablespoon chopped fresh parsley

Big pinch cayenne pepper

½ cup Creole or regular cream cheese, softened

16 slices pickled jalapeño

8 strips thick-cut smoked bacon, halved and blanched

Preheat the broiler. Season the duck strips with salt and pepper and lay out on a platter. In a bowl, mix the thyme, parsley, and cayenne into the softened cream cheese; add salt and pepper. Put a slice of jalapeño on each duck strip, then spoon on ½ tablespoon of seasoned cream cheese. Wrap each strip around the filling, then wrap a piece of bacon around the duck. Secure the poppers on skewers.

Broil the skewers until the bacon is crispy and slightly charred, turning once. Serve immediately.

My Chef Chris Kerageorgiou was a Provençal cook famous for coaxing the most flavor from the humblest ingredients. He taught me this super easy pâté when I worked for him at La Provence, the restaurant we're now lucky enough to own in Lacombe, Louisiana. I like to serve the pâté with thinly sliced toasts.

Chef Chris's Chicken Liver Pâté

✦ Serves 10-12

2 cups chicken livers	Pinch pepper
2 eggs	1 tablespoon salt
½ tablespoon celery salt	1½ cups hot melted butter
½ tablespoon garlic powder	
½ tablespoon onion powder	

Preheat the oven to 300°. Put all the ingredients except the butter into a blender. While blending, slowly pour in the melted butter until the mixture is very smooth.

Transfer the mixture to a small baking dish and set that dish in a pan filled with hot water to come halfway up the sides. Bake for 30-45 minutes until the pâté is firm in the center.

Let cool, then refrigerate for at least 2 hours before serving.

Chapter 2
SOUPS & BISQUES

Everything that I see and smell, cook and eat, reminds me of where I come from and more or less dictates where I'm going. Carcasses and bones, peelings and shells are flavor boosters. I save the carcass of every bird I roast and freeze it for the next stock. Sautéing the shells of shrimp, crab, and crawfish is the secret to the nutty flavor of a good rich bisque.

 I love soup and I especially love to make variations on the classic base of leeks and potatoes, this time by adding cauliflower. You can use just about any vegetable. Or make a simple potato and leek soup, and serve it chilled for a great vichyssoise. 〞

Creamy Cauliflower Soup

✦ Serves 8

¼ cup olive oil

1 whole leek, trimmed and chopped

1 head cauliflower, trimmed and chopped

2 cloves garlic, minced

1 large potato, peeled and roughly chopped

4 cups Go-To Chicken Stock (recipe follows)

½ cup cream

Salt and pepper

Heat the oil in a large heavy-bottomed pot over medium-high heat and sweat the leeks and cauliflower, stirring, for about 2 minutes. Add the garlic and cook 2 minutes more. You want a white soup, so don't let the vegetables brown.

Add the potatoes, stock, and cream. Bring to a boil, then reduce immediately to a simmer. The potatoes will become soft and silky in about 20 minutes.

Transfer the soup to a blender and puree. I have a tendency to blow this up from time to time, so make sure not to overfill the blender and blend on low speed. Add salt and pepper.

Go-To Chicken Stock

Making stock is not complicated. I freeze the carcasses from every chicken I roast and make stock when I have enough of them. I start by putting the carcasses in a stockpot. Often I'll brown some chicken and/or turkey wings in the oven (about 1 pound of bones total), and throw them into the pot as well. I then add a couple of chopped carrots and celery stalks along with a few cloves of crushed garlic and a couple of bay leaves. Then I pour in enough cool water to cover the bones by a few inches and bring to a boil. Then simply simmer for about 2 hours. Strain it all and you're done. (And remember, in a pinch, do as so many New Orleans home cooks do: use water.)

VARIATIONS

To make Fish Stock, use 1 pound fish heads and bones instead of the chicken.

For Shellfish Stock, use 1 pound shells from shrimp, blue crab, crawfish, or lobster.

For Shrimp Stock, use 1 pound shrimp heads and shells.

For Crab Stock, use 1 pound crab shells.

My Grandmother Grace always served a big lunch and, always, supper was usually just a good soup and sandwich. So making soup always makes me think of her. I like to make soup with our big green-and-white-striped Southern heirloom cushaw squash, right. Its flavor is light, like summer squash—which is another great option for this soup. I serve the soup with brown shrimp from Lake Pontchartrain. Mmm, mmm, mmm!

White Squash & Shrimp Soup

✦ Serves 6

4 tablespoons butter	1 sprig fresh thyme
1 onion, chopped	6 cups Go-To Chicken Stock or Shrimp Stock (page 27)
1 leek, trimmed and chopped	2 cups heavy cream
1 stalk celery, chopped	Pinch cayenne pepper
3 cloves garlic, minced	Pinch allspice
3 cups peeled, diced white or other summer squash	Salt and pepper
1 medium Yukon Gold potato, peeled and sliced	1 pound medium wild American shrimp, peeled and deveined
1 bay leaf	1 green onion, chopped

Melt the butter in a medium pot over medium heat. Add the onions, leeks, celery, and garlic and cook for several minutes. Add the squash and potatoes and cook, stirring occasionally, until slightly softened, 5–10 minutes.

Add the bay leaf, thyme, stock, and cream to the pot and bring to a boil over medium-high heat. Lower the heat and simmer the soup for 15–20 minutes.

Remove and discard the bay leaf and thyme. Puree the soup in a blender until smooth. Strain it if you like, but I appreciate a bit of texture here. Return the soup to the pot and add the cayenne, allspice, salt, and pepper. Toss the shrimp with salt and pepper and add them with the green onions to the pot. Simmer the soup for 5 minutes more and then serve.

This soup's character comes from the shrimp heads and shells. Toasted, as in the photograph, they're even more flavorful than the shrimp themselves. But a generous shot of Armagnac doesn't hurt.

Shrimp & Armagnac Bisque

✦ Serves 8-10

¼ cup olive oil
2 dozen medium wild American shrimp, peeled and deveined, heads and shells reserved
¼ cup flour
1 onion, chopped
1 stalk celery, chopped
¼ bell pepper, chopped
4 cloves garlic, minced
1 sprig fresh thyme
1 teaspoon dried tarragon

1 bay leaf
2 teaspoons crushed red pepper flakes
¼ cup Armagnac or other brandy
6 cups Shrimp Stock (page 27) or water
2 cups heavy cream
Big dash Worcestershire
Big dash Tabasco
Salt and pepper

Heat the oil in a large heavy-bottomed pot over high heat. Add the shrimp heads and shells and cook, stirring frequently, for 10 minutes. Add the flour and stir in well, then add the onions, celery, bell pepper, and garlic. Lower the heat to medium and cook for 15 minutes more. Add the thyme, tarragon, bay leaf, and pepper flakes, stir well, and cook for another 5 minutes.

Add the Armagnac and shrimp and cook, stirring, for several minutes. Stir in the shrimp stock and heavy cream, raise the heat to medium high, and bring to a boil. Lower the heat to a slow simmer and cook for 25 minutes more. Remove from the heat and discard the thyme sprig and bay leaf.

Puree the bisque in a blender. Strain into bowls, season well with Worcestershire, Tabasco, salt, and pepper, and serve.

Toasting the crab shells is the most important part of good bisques; that's the way to develop the rich, nutty flavor they are famous for. The farther west you go in Louisiana, the less cream and the more rice you'll find in your bisque.

Creole Crab Bisque

✦ Serves 6–8

¼ cup olive oil	1 sprig fresh thyme
8 blue crabs, quartered	1 bay leaf
2 tablespoons flour	1 teaspoon crushed red pepper flakes
1 onion, chopped	¼ cup brandy
1 stalk celery, chopped	2 cups heavy cream
4 cloves garlic, crushed	Tabasco
¼ cup white rice, crushed in a mortar	Salt and pepper
1 tablespoon tomato paste	

Heat the oil in a large heavy-bottomed pot over high heat. Crush the crabs and add to the pot with their juices. Cook, stirring frequently, for 15 minutes. Stir in the flour then add the onions, celery, and garlic. Lower the heat to medium and cook for 15 minutes more. Add the rice, tomato paste, thyme, bay leaf, and pepper flakes, stir well, and cook for another 5 minutes.

Add the brandy and cook, stirring, for several minutes more. Stir in 6 cups water and the heavy cream, raise the heat, and bring to a boil. Lower the heat to a slow simmer and cook for 25 minutes more. Remove from the heat and discard the thyme sprig and bay leaf.

Puree the bisque in a blender. Strain into bowls, season with Tabasco, salt, and pepper, and serve.

VARIATION

Cajun Crawfish Bisque

This is such a simple, easy happy soup to make if you can get your hands on some whole fresh crawfish. (In season, order them from Kenney's Seafood, 985-643-2717.) Use the Creole Crab Bisque recipe (above), substituting 2 pounds whole crawfish for the crabs. I like to shell a handful of cooked crawfish to top each bowl, as in the photograph.

When the spirit absinthe was banned in this country in the early 1900s (due to its high alcoholic content and overindulgence by controversial avant-garde poets and writers), a New Orleans company approximated its anise flavor and produced the liqueur Herbsaint, so crucial in our Sazerac cocktail. I love the way Herbsaint enhances this soup.

Oyster, Artichoke & Herbsaint Soup

✦ Serves 6

4 tablespoons butter	2 dozen oysters, shucked, with their liquor (about ½ cup)
1 onion, chopped	Hearts and stems of 4 artichokes, trimmed, chopped, and reserved in lemon water
1 leek, white and pale green parts, chopped	
4 cloves garlic, minced	
4 tablespoons flour	Juice of 1 lemon
⅓ cup Herbsaint	Tabasco
1 cup cream	Salt and pepper
3 cups Go-To Chicken Stock (page 27)	2 big handfuls spinach, washed and chopped

Melt the butter in a large skillet and cook the onions, leeks, and garlic until soft. Whisk in the flour and continue to whisk over medium-high heat for another couple of minutes, just until a light roux comes together.

Slowly stir in the Herbsaint, cream, stock, and oyster liquor until the liquid comes to a boil, then add the artichoke hearts and stems. Lower the heat to a simmer and cook for 15 minutes.

Add the lemon juice, Tabasco, salt, and pepper.

Just a few minutes before serving, stir in the spinach and the oysters. Heat just until the spinach wilts and the oysters begin to curl, then serve.

❝ The name of this country turn on the classic Italian Wedding soup, left, is an example of the level of our sense of humor! Our version is a combination of ingredients that really do marry together happily. This soup is hearty enough to be a meal. ❞

❝ Our tomato season lasts from as early as March till as late as November. I put up plenty of tomato sauce during the season so we can make this soup, chilled or hot, all year long. You can too. ❞

Divorce Soup

✦ Serves 6

1 tablespoon bacon fat or oil	1 cup chopped tomatoes
1 pound Italian sausage, removed from casings	2 quarts Go-To Chicken Stock (page 27)
1 onion, minced	1 teaspoon dried oregano
4 cloves garlic, minced	2 cups cooked field peas or other cooked dried beans
1 teaspoon crushed red pepper flakes	Salt and pepper
2 handfuls mustard greens, turnip greens, or kale, chopped	

Heat the bacon fat in a large heavy-bottomed pot over medium-high heat. Wet your hands a bit and roll the sausage meat into small meatballs. Brown the meatballs quickly in the bacon fat, then add the onions, garlic, and pepper flakes. Cook a few minutes more until the onions soften.

Add the greens, tomatoes, stock, and oregano and bring to a boil. Then add the field peas, salt, and pepper and cook until the soup is hot. Remove from the heat. Divide the meatballs among 6 soup bowls, ladle in the soup, and serve with corn bread (page 129).

Creole Tomato Soup

✦ Serves 8

¼ cup olive oil	2 teaspoons crushed red pepper flakes
4 cloves garlic, crushed	3 sprigs fresh basil, chopped
1 leek, trimmed and chopped	Sugar
2 quarts Cherry Tomato Five-Minute Sauce (page 84)	Salt
1 cup heavy cream	

Heat the oil in a large, heavy-bottomed pot over high heat. Add the garlic and leeks and stir a minute, but don't let them brown. Add the tomato sauce, cream, pepper flakes, and basil and bring to a boil. Transfer to a blender and puree. Add a little sugar to balance the tartness, and a big pinch of salt.

Nothing beats the woodsy, peppery aroma of the chanterelles we find growing wild on the sandy river bluffs on the North Shore of Lake Pontchartrain. If you happen to live elsewhere, use whatever mushrooms you can find; wild are always tastier.

Honey Island Chanterelle Soup

✦ Serves 6

¼ cup olive oil	1 teaspoon crushed red pepper flakes
1 onion, chopped	1 sprig fresh thyme
1 head green garlic or 3 green onions, minced	1 cup white wine
1 pound chanterelle mushrooms, chopped	3 cups Go-To Chicken Stock (page 27)
1 small russet potato, peeled and chopped	1 cup heavy cream
	Salt and pepper

Heat the oil in a large heavy-bottomed pot over medium heat. Add the onions and garlic and cook, stirring often, until the onions are translucent, about 5 minutes. Raise the heat to medium high and add the chanterelles. Cook, stirring, for 5 minutes.

Add the potatoes, pepper flakes, thyme, and white wine to the pot. Cook for several minutes until the wine has reduced by half. Add the chicken stock and cream and, when the soup comes to a boil, reduce the heat to medium low. Cover and simmer until the potatoes are tender, about 20 minutes.

Add salt and pepper. If the soup seems a bit thick, add a little water or stock.

Chapter 3
STEW POT

❝ New Orleans embraced its slow cooking long before that became fashionable. We can spend all day cooking the good stuff—the étouffées, the courtbouillons, the grillades and the gravies. As a kid, if I brought home a redfish, you'd better believe my mother would slow-cook it whole in a broth perfumed by onion, garlic, celery, bay leaves, allspice, Creole tomatoes, cayenne pepper, and a pinch of dried thyme. If it was an extra special evening, crabmeat, shrimp, or oysters could end up in her courtbouillon. And that's how I make courtbouillon today. ❞

TURNING
VEHICLES
YIELD

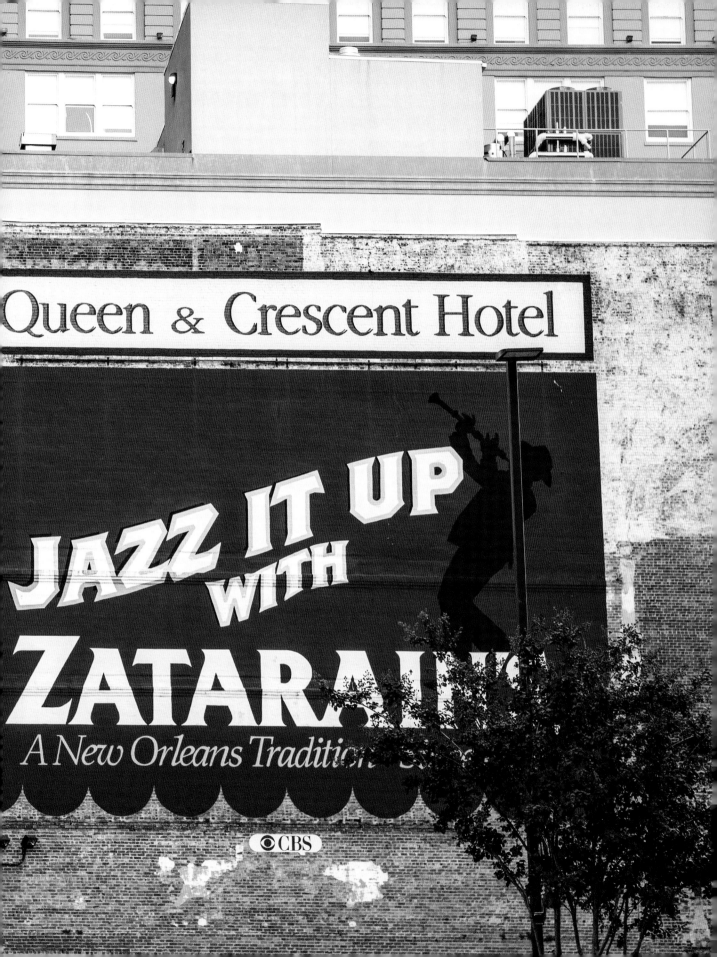

❝ Alon Shaya is chef of our Italian restaurant, Domenica; Pizza Domenica; and now, Shaya, our modern Israeli restaurant. I love his masterful way with braised rabbit. ❞

Alon's Rabbit Daube

✦ Makes 4 servings

3 tablespoons olive oil	1 cup canned tomatoes
1 4-pound rabbit, quartered	2 ounces dried wild mushrooms
Salt and pepper	1 teaspoon dried thyme
1 onion, chopped	Pinch crushed red pepper flakes
1 stalk celery, chopped	1 bay leaf
1 large carrot, chopped	Handful whole baby carrots, peeled and trimmed
3 cloves garlic, minced	
3 tablespoons flour	2 green onions, chopped
2 cups Go-To Chicken Stock (page 27)	Rice, for serving
½ cup white wine	

Heat the oil in a medium heavy-bottomed pot over medium-high heat. Season the rabbit with salt and pepper and sear until browned all over.

Add the onions, celery, chopped carrot, and garlic to the pot and cook, stirring frequently, for 5 minutes or so. Dust with the flour and stir it in for 3 minutes. Add the stock, wine, tomatoes, mushrooms, thyme, pepper flakes, and bay leaf. Bring to a boil, then reduce the heat to medium low. Simmer until the rabbit is fork-tender and the meat is nearly falling off the bones, about 1 hour. Turn the rabbit pieces every so often to ensure that they cook evenly and toss in the whole baby carrots after about a half hour.

Season with salt and pepper. Discard the bay leaf. Serve over rice with the chopped green onions.

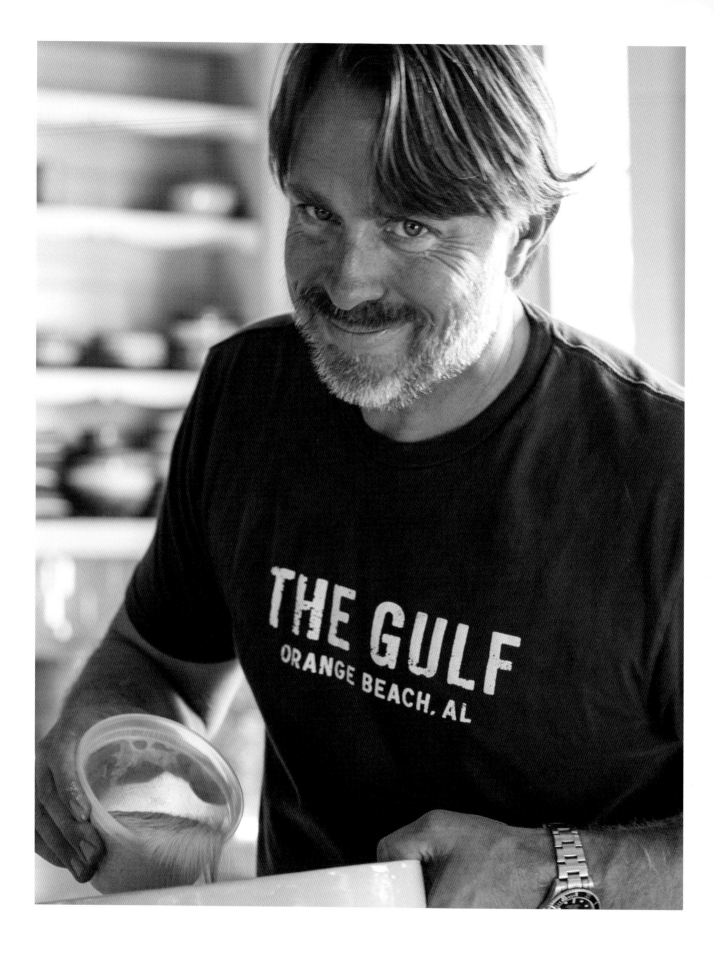

STEW POT

❝ Think of grillades as a Creole-style pot roast made with slices of pork, veal, beef, or, when it's hunting season, venison. For this down-home stew I use pork shoulder, aka Boston butt, cut against the grain into thin-ish slices. Sometimes I even make grillades from thick slices of roasted pork, just browning the cutlets well on both sides. Make grillades ahead of time; they're so easy to reheat. I love to serve them over Baked Cheesy Grits (page 124). ❞

Mardi Gras Morning Pork Shoulder Grillades

✦ Serves 6

2-3 pounds pork or beef cutlets, pounded thin	¼ cup flour
Salt and pepper	1 cup chopped tomatoes
1 teaspoon dried thyme	1 teaspoon crushed red pepper flakes
Flour for dusting	1 teaspoon dried oregano
¼ cup olive oil	2 cups Go-To Chicken Stock (page 27) or beef broth
1 onion, chopped	Grits, for serving
3 cloves garlic, minced	

Season the cutlets with salt, pepper, and the thyme. Dust with flour and sauté in the olive oil in a large skillet over high heat, browning on both sides. As they brown, remove the grillades to a platter. Add the onions to the skillet and cook, stirring, for about 7 minutes or until browned.

When the onions have browned, add the garlic and dust the onion mixture with the ¼ cup flour. Stir for 3 minutes over high heat, then add the tomatoes and pepper flakes. Bring to a boil and add the oregano and stock. Return to a boil, stirring constantly, and season well with salt and pepper. Return the grillades to the skillet and lower the heat to a simmer. Cover and cook for at least 5 minutes.

Serve a generous portion of grits on each plate, then top with grillades and lots of gravy.

ff The key is to sear
the meat uniformly on all
sides before proceeding
with the recipe. Once the
meat is perfectly seared,
remove it from the pot,
add the onions and
caramelize them, stirring
until they turn a rich
mahogany color. Now you
have the building blocks
for this great stew. **JJ**

Beef Brisket Daube

✦ Serves 6

4	pounds beef brisket, cut into 2-inch cubes	2	cups red wine
	Salt and pepper	1	cup diced tomatoes
¼	cup canola oil	2	cups Go-To Chicken Stock (page 27) or beef broth
1	onion, chopped	2	ounces dried wild mushrooms
1	stalk celery, chopped	1	tablespoon dried thyme
1	carrot, chopped	2	bay leaves
4	cloves garlic, minced		

Season the brisket with salt and pepper. Heat the oil in a large heavy-bottomed pot over high heat. Add the meat, several pieces at a time. Stir and turn the meat often, carefully letting each piece brown before removing it from the pot. Reserve browned meat.

Add the onions, celery, carrot, and garlic to the pot. Stirring constantly, let the vegetables cook until the onions turn deep brown. Then return the beef to the pot along with the wine, tomatoes, stock, mushrooms, thyme, and bay leaves. Bring to a boil then lower the heat and cover. Let the stew cook until the meat is fork tender, about 2 hours.

Once the beef is cooked, discard the bay leaves and season the braising liquid with salt and pepper. Serve hot, right out of the pot, over rice, pasta, or potatoes.

Don't crowd the pot when you brown the chicken thighs. If you do you'll ultimately steam the chicken, not brown it; it'll take longer and have less flavor. If you do take your time browning the chicken, it will pay off in deliciousness.

Chicken Thigh Fricassee

✦ Serves 4-6

Salt and pepper
8 chicken thighs
3 tablespoons olive oil
1 onion, chopped
8 ounces mushrooms, sliced
1 stalk celery, chopped
4 cloves garlic, thinly sliced
1 12-ounce can diced tomatoes

2 quarts Go-To Chicken Stock (page 27)
2 teaspoons dried thyme
6 baby turnips, peeled
10 baby carrots, peeled
10 fingerling potatoes, halved
3 green onions, chopped

Generously salt and pepper the chicken thighs. Heat the oil in a large heavy-bottomed pot over high heat. Add the chicken and brown on all sides, 2-3 minutes per side. Remove the chicken from the pot and reserve.

Add the onions to the pot and cook to soften, then add the mushrooms, celery, and garlic. Cook until the mixture turns a rich brown, about 5 minutes. Add the tomatoes, stirring frequently, and cook for 3 minutes more.

Lower the heat to medium and add the chicken stock and thyme. Return the chicken to the pot and bring to a simmer. Cover and simmer the stew over low heat for 30 minutes. Add the turnips, carrots, and potatoes. Cover and cook for additional 30 minutes, until the chicken is fork-tender and the thigh bones are loose. Top with the green onions and serve.

Mr. Paul's Pintail en Daube

✦ Serves 6-8

- 4 pintail or mallard ducks, cleaned and quartered
- 1 tablespoon herbes de Provence
  Salt and pepper
- ¼ cup bacon fat or oil
- 2 onions, chopped
- 1 carrot, chopped

- 1 stalk celery, chopped
- 1 cup mushrooms, chopped
- 4 cloves garlic, thinly sliced
- 4 tablespoons flour
- 1 tablespoon tomato paste
- 2 cups port wine
- 2 cups Go-To Chicken Stock (page 27)

- Big pinch crushed red pepper flakes
- 1 bay leaf
  Tabasco
- 2 green onions, chopped
  Rice, for serving

> I was lucky enough to know and to hunt with Mr. Paul McIlhenny, who started working at his family's famed Avery Island–based Tabasco company in 1967. If we had a great duck hunt, Mr. Paul would cook us up this stew.

Season the ducks all over with the herbes de Provence, salt, and pepper. Heat the bacon fat in a heavy-bottomed pot over a high heat. Add the duck and sear on all sides until browned. Remove the duck from the pot but reserve the drippings.

Reduce the heat to medium high, add the onions, and cook until they turn mahogany brown. Add the carrot, celery, mushrooms, and garlic. Continue to cook and stir until the vegetables have softened, about 3 minutes. Add the flour and stir for another 3–5 minutes, then stir in the tomato paste.

Add the wine, stock, pepper flakes, and bay leaf. Raise the heat, bring to a boil, and return the duck to the pot. Reduce the heat, cover, and simmer for about 1½ hours, until the duck nearly pulls away from the bone. Season with salt and pepper and, of course, Tabasco. Top with green onions and serve over rice.

"" Caldo, a variation of the Spanish vegetable stew called *puchero*, came to us from our Canary Island relatives, the Isleños, who were sent by the king of Spain in the late 1700s to settle St. Bernard Parish, southeast of New Orleans. It's a big vegetable stew cooked in a big cauldron (caldo), its base of onion, bell pepper, and celery is what we call the 'holy trinity,' but the Isleños knew it as the Spanish sofrito. Add beans, sweet potatoes, or whatever's fresh. ""

Summer Vegetable Caldo

✦ Serves 8–10

3 tablespoons olive oil	1 cup chopped tomatoes
1 large onion, chopped	1 cup corn kernels
1 bell pepper, chopped	1 carrot, peeled and chopped
1 stalk celery, chopped	3 quarts Go-To Chicken Stock (page 27) or water
4 cloves garlic, minced	2 bay leaves
½ cup chopped salt pork or bacon, or 1 ham hock	1 teaspoon cayenne pepper
1 cup okra	Salt and pepper
2 large handfuls mustard greens, chopped	

Heat the oil in a large heavy-bottomed pot over medium heat. Add the onions, bell pepper, celery, and garlic and soften, about 5 minutes. Add the salt pork, cook a minute or two to begin releasing the fat, then add all the fresh vegetables.

Add the stock, bay leaves, cayenne, salt, and pepper. Bring to a boil over high heat, then reduce to a gentle simmer and cook just until all the vegetables are tender. You still want to be able to identify each one. Caldo's all about that fresh vegetable flavor.

❝ Leroy Phillips was an iconic character down in St. Bernard Parish who taught me this Oyster Stew. He grew up in the marshes without electricity, fishing off the back of his shrimp boat. **❞**

Leroy's Oyster Stew

✦ Serves 6

> **Leroy was a country cook with Isleño roots, and proud of it. Fat local oysters and the pan sauce made from their liquor are the secrets of this stew.**

1 leek, white part, minced	Pinch dried thyme
3 cloves garlic, minced	3 dozen oysters, shucked and liquor reserved for Pan Sauce
1 tablespoon olive oil	
1 large tomato, chopped	Tabasco
2 green onions, chopped	Squeeze of lemon juice
Go-To Oyster Pan Sauce (opposite)	Salt and pepper

Cook the leeks and garlic in the oil in a large saucepan over medium heat until softened, about 3 minutes. Add the tomatoes, green onions, oyster pan sauce, and thyme, increase the heat to high, and bring to a boil. Lower the heat to a simmer, add the oysters, and cook just until they become firm and their edges begin to curl. Season with Tabasco, lemon juice, salt, and pepper, and stir to combine the flavors.

Green Onion Sausage & Shrimp Stew

✦ Serves 6-8

- 1 pound green-onion pork sausage, removed from casings
- 1 tablespoon bacon fat or oil
- 1 onion, chopped
- 1 tablespoon flour
- 1 pound jumbo wild American shrimp, peeled and deveined
  Salt and pepper
- ½ jalapeño pepper, seeds removed, minced
- 1 clove garlic, minced
- 1 cup canned diced tomatoes
  Pinch allspice
  Big dash Worcestershire
- 1 cup Go-To Chicken Stock (page 27)
- 1 teaspoon dried thyme
- 1 green onion, chopped

Render the sausage in the bacon fat in a large skillet over high heat. Once the sausage has browned, add the onions and cook until deep brown. Lower the heat to medium high and add the flour, stirring frequently.

Season the shrimp with salt and pepper, stir them into the pan, and cook for 3 minutes. Stir in the jalapeño and garlic. Remove the shrimp from the pan (so they don't overcook) and reserve, then add the tomatoes, allspice, and Worcestershire. Stir well, raise the heat, then add the stock and thyme and bring to a boil.

Lower the heat to medium low and cook for 15 minutes. Return the shrimp to the pan along with the green onions and let the shrimp cook for another 5 minutes. Add salt and pepper and serve.

> ❝❝ In South Louisiana, we can readily get our hands on green onion sausage. If you can't find it, don't worry. Just use pork sausage and an extra handful of chopped green onions. ❞❞

Go-To Oyster Pan Sauce

✦ Makes about 3 cups

The rich flavor of this stew comes from a simple oyster pan sauce. I make it by heating some olive oil in a skillet with a diced large onion, a minced fennel bulb, 4 minced garlic cloves, a heaping teaspoon each crushed red pepper flakes, thyme, and tarragon, and 2 bay leaves. Once the vegetables have softened, I add 1½ cups heavy cream, 1½ cups dry vermouth, and 3 cups oyster liquor or water. Increase the heat to high and reduce the sauce by half, about 15 minutes. For a **Shellfish Pan Sauce,** just substitute **Shellfish Stock** (page 27) for the oyster liquor.

 Gracie was the great New Orleans cook for a friend's family, and this is the wonderful stew she'd effortlessly cook up in an old copper pot. Anything with crabmeat in it is just so darn good. ⁊⁊

Gracie's Crab & Sausage Stew

✦ Serves 6-8

½ cup canola oil
½ cup flour
1 onion, chopped
6 blue crabs, opened, gills removed, cut into 4 pieces each
1 pound smoked sausage, sliced ½ inch thick
1 stalk celery, chopped
2 cloves garlic, minced

6 cups Shellfish Stock (page 27)
2 bay leaves
1 pound crabmeat
   Dash Worcestershire
   Dash Tabasco
   Salt and pepper
4-6 cups cooked white rice
2 green onions, sliced

Make a roux by heating the oil in a large heavy-bottomed pot over high heat. Whisk the flour into the hot oil. It will immediately begin to sizzle. Reduce the heat to medium and continue whisking until the roux turns a deep brown color, about 15 minutes. Add the onions, stirring them into the roux with a wooden spoon. Lower the heat to medium low and continue stirring until the roux turns a glossy dark brown, about 10 minutes.

Add the crabs and sausage and stir for a minute, then add the celery and garlic. Raise the heat to medium and stir for about 3 minutes. Add the shellfish stock and bay leaves. Bring the stew to a boil, stirring occasionally. Reduce the heat and simmer for 45 minutes, stirring occasionally and skimming off the fat with a spoon.

Remove and discard the bay leaves. Add the crabmeat, then season well with Worcestershire, Tabasco, salt, and pepper. Serve over white rice and scatter green onions on top.

Brown Shrimp & Okra Stew

✦ Serves 6

6 large handfuls fresh okra, stem ends trimmed
2 tablespoons baking soda
Salt
2 cups chopped tomatoes
¼ cup diced bell pepper
4 cloves garlic, thinly sliced
¼ cup olive oil
1 teaspoon crushed red pepper flakes
1 teaspoon sugar
2 pounds medium wild American shrimp, peeled and deveined
1 teaspoon dried oregano
Pepper
3 cups cooked white rice
2 green onions, chopped

Bring a gallon of water to a boil in a large pot. Add the okra, baking soda, and 2 tablespoons salt and cook at a hard boil for 5 minutes. Transfer the okra with a slotted spoon to a bowl of ice water. After a minute, drain the okra and reserve.

Cook the tomatoes, bell pepper, and garlic together in the oil in a medium skillet over medium-high heat for several minutes. Add the pepper flakes and sugar and cook, stirring constantly, for 10 minutes. Add the okra, shrimp, and oregano. Reduce the heat to medium low and cook for another 3–4 minutes. Season with salt and pepper. Spoon over rice and scatter green onions on top.

❝ Okra is so, so good with the quickly cooked shrimp. I like to make this stew when I can find plenty of really small, fresh okra in the market. I cook the okra with some baking soda, then shock the cooked okra in ice water to preserve its bright green color. ❞

❝ The gracious Pontalba Buildings, built in the 1840s on Jackson Square in the Quarter, say New Orleans to me. **❞**

❝ This is such a simple, iconic Louisiana partnership: our wild Gulf shrimp served over excellent grits. The quality of the shrimp really matters here, because they're not cooked long, just quickly sautéed in olive oil. After the shrimp are briefly cooked, they're removed from the skillet and returned just when the light sauce is ready to be ladled over the grits. **❞**

Duck Camp Shrimp & Grits

✦ Serves 6

2 tablespoons olive oil
30 jumbo wild American shrimp, peeled and deveined
  Salt
1 cup sliced andouille or other smoked pork sausage
1 pound fresh pork sausage, casings removed
1 onion, chopped
3 cloves garlic, minced

1 teaspoon dried thyme
4 cups Shrimp Stock (page 27)
2 cups diced tomatoes
1 teaspoon fresh lemon juice
2 green onions, chopped
  Baked Cheesy Grits (page 124)

Heat the oil in a large skillet over medium heat. Season the shrimp with salt and sauté until they start to brown but are not cooked all the way through. Remove the shrimp and set aside.

In the same pan, sauté the smoked sausage, crumbled pork sausage, onions, garlic, and thyme until they become aromatic, about 5 minutes. Add the stock and bring to a simmer. Reduce the sauce until it is nice and thick, 3–5 minutes. Return the shrimp to the skillet and cook another 5 minutes. Add the diced tomatoes and lemon juice.

Serve the shrimp in a big tureen topped with the green onions, with the grits on the side.

Drew's Catfish Courtbouillon

✦ Serves 6

8	tablespoons butter
½	cup flour
1	onion, chopped
1	stalk celery, chopped
1	bell pepper, chopped
1	clove garlic, thinly sliced
2	cups canned crushed tomatoes

3	cups Shellfish Stock (page 27)
1	cup dry white wine
1	teaspoon crushed red pepper flakes
	Big pinch ground allspice
2-3	pounds fresh catfish filets, cut into 3-inch pieces
½	pound crabmeat

1	handful fresh parsley, chopped
2	sprigs tarragon, chopped
	Salt and pepper
	Tabasco
	Worcestershire
3	green onions, sliced

❝ My good friend Drew Mire would cook this up if you just looked at him the right way. Courtbouillon (pronounced CU-boo-yon) is our New Orleans tomato-based fish stew and can take so many different forms and ingredients. Here's Drew's easy, oh-so delicious version with catfish and crab. ❞

Make a blond roux in a large heavy-bottomed pot over medium-high heat by melting the butter and stirring in the flour. Cook and stir for about 3 minutes then add the onions, celery, bell pepper, and garlic. Cook until the vegetables are soft, 5–7 minutes.

Add the tomatoes, stock, wine, pepper flakes, and allspice. Raise the heat to high and continue to stir until the liquid comes to a boil. Lower the heat to a simmer, cover the pot, and cook for about 30 minutes.

Add the fish, crabmeat, parsley, and tarragon, then raise the heat and cook for another 6 minutes. Just before serving in big bowls, add salt, pepper, Tabasco, and Worcestershire, and top with green onions.

GUMBO

> Gumbo is our Jesse Tree, the footprint of who we are and where we come from. It's a cultural stew: Africans gave us *kingombo*, their word for okra; Native Americans dried and powdered sassafras leaves for the thickener called *filé*. The French brought us their fat and flour base called roux; the Spanish their sofrito–what we call the 'holy trinity'–onion, celery, and bell pepper. Germans gave us smoked sausages, and the Caribbeans, their bright spices.

GUMBO

When I say I cook at home more and more like my mother and grandmother did, this gumbo is a great example. Cooking it makes me so happy! I get that deep shellfish flavor from cooking the crabs at least 45 minutes before adding the other seafood. It's all about tasting, adjusting the flavors, and really just cooking from your heart. 🔊🔊

Mamma's Seafood Gumbo

✦ Serves 10

¾ cup canola oil
¾ cup flour
2 large onions, chopped
6 blue crabs, quartered
1 stalk celery, chopped
4 cloves garlic, minced
3 quarts Shrimp or Shellfish Stock (page 27)
2 cups sliced okra
1 tablespoon fresh or dried thyme
2 bay leaves
1 pound smoked sausage, sliced ½ inch thick

4 green onions, chopped
2 tablespoons from My Creole Spice Jar (page xi)
Salt and pepper
Tabasco
1 pound medium wild American shrimp, peeled and deveined
1 pint shucked oysters and their liquor
1 cup crabmeat
6 cups white rice

Make a roux by heating the oil in a large heavy-bottomed pot over high heat. Whisk the flour into the hot oil. It will immediately begin to sizzle. Reduce the heat to medium and continue whisking until the roux turns a deep brown color, about 15 minutes. Add the onions, stirring them into the roux with a wooden spoon. Lower the heat to medium low and continue stirring until the roux turns a glossy dark brown, about 10 minutes.

Add the blue crabs and stir for a minute to toast the shells, then add the celery and garlic. Raise the heat to medium and cook, stirring, for 3 minutes. Add the stock, okra, thyme, and bay leaves. Bring the gumbo to a boil, stirring occasionally. Reduce the heat to medium low and simmer for 45 minutes. Stir occasionally and skim off the fat from the surface of the gumbo (moving the pot half off the burner helps collect the impurities).

Add the sausage and green onions to the pot and cook for 15 minutes. Season well with the Creole spices, salt, pepper, and Tabasco. Add the shrimp, oysters and their liquor, and crabmeat to the pot and cook for about 5 minutes. Serve with rice.

Secrets of Roux

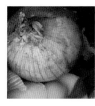

I've probably cooked nine thousand gumbos in my life and I've acquired a bit of wisdom on how to make the legendary stew base called roux. Just about any fat works: I love rendered duck fat, chicken fat, or bacon fat, but canola oil works nearly as well. Instead of adding the fat and flour to the pot at the same time, I start by heating up the fat and wait for its heat to waft up from the pot. Then I add the flour (always 1 part fat, 1 part flour) and let it bubble up and fry a bit. I use a whisk to emulsify the flour into the fat. A spoon just won't cut it fast enough. As I whisk, I watch the brown spots of flour disappear into the fat. As soon as the roux starts to smell like roasted pecans, I turn the heat down, so I don't burn the roux. You can't take your eyes off that pot: watch and smell the roux as it thickens and darkens. Keep stirring so nothing sticks. Once the roux turns a milk chocolate color, it's time to add the chopped onions. As the onions mix with the roux, you'll see it become glossier as the sugars in the onions start to caramelize, becoming sweeter and super intense. The roux will darken even more, and only now can you think about adding the other ingredients.

GUMBO

How you make your gumbo depends on where you come from. Those of us within eyesight of New Orleans like the rich, deep flavor of a Creole gumbo. We use tomatoes and/or tomato paste, which you'd never see in a gumbo from Cajun country. And for me, it's not a real gumbo without okra; fresh is better, but out of season, frozen is okay.

Chicken & Sausage Gumbo

✦ Serves 10

¾ cup chicken fat or canola oil
¾ cup flour
2 large onions, chopped
1 large chicken, cut into 12 pieces
2 tablespoons from My Creole Spice Jar (page xi)
2 pounds spicy smoked sausage, sliced ½ inch thick
2 stalks celery, chopped
2 green bell peppers, seeded and chopped
1 tomato, seeded and chopped

3 cloves garlic, minced
3 quarts Go-To Chicken Stock (page 27)
1 tablespoon dried thyme
2 bay leaves
6 ounces andouille sausage, roughly chopped
2 cups sliced okra
1 tablespoon Worcestershire
Tabasco
Salt and pepper
6 cups cooked white rice

Make a roux by heating the fat in a large heavy-bottomed pot over high heat. Whisk the flour into the hot fat. It will immediately begin to sizzle. Reduce the heat to medium and continue whisking until the roux turns a deep brown color, about 15 minutes. Add the onions, stirring them into the roux with a wooden spoon. Lower the heat to medium low and continue stirring until the roux turns a glossy dark brown, about 10 minutes.

Season the chicken pieces with the Creole spices and add the chicken to the hot roux. Once the chicken is well-seared, add the smoked sausage and stir well. Then add the celery, bell peppers, tomatoes, and garlic. Raise the heat to medium high, stir for another 3 minutes or so, then add the stock, thyme, and bay leaves.

Bring the gumbo to a boil while stirring, then reduce the heat to medium low and let simmer for 45 minutes. Stir occasionally and skim the fat from the surface of the gumbo (moving the pot half off the burner helps collect the impurities).

Add the andouille sausage, okra, and Worcestershire, season well with Tabasco, salt, and pepper, and simmer for another 45 minutes. Skim the gumbo before serving with the white rice.

Smoked pork sausage (left) and andouille give our gumbos and stews that smoky essence that I love. I can't imagine gumbo without them.

❝ I duck hunt with the same group of guys I've hunted with for decades and we still argue about whose gumbo is best. It just might be Mr. Paul's Duck, Andouille & Oyster Gumbo. ❞

❝ I would cook this gumbo quite often with Mr. Paul McIlhenny, who ran his family's Tabasco company. This is a great example of the brothier style of gumbo preferred out west in Avery Island. I love how the dry, spicy, andouille sausage perfumes the stew. Our plump oysters add a touch of brininess at the end. It's Southern Louisiana in a bowl. ❞

Mr. Paul's Duck, Andouille & Oyster Gumbo

✦ Serves 10

¾ cup canola oil	4 cloves garlic, minced
¾ cup flour	4 green onions, chopped
3 large onions, chopped	4 quarts Go-To Chicken Stock (page 27)
1 large domestic duck or 3 wild ducks, cut into quarters	2 bay leaves
Salt and pepper	1 pound andouille sausage, roughly chopped
2 pounds smoked sausage, sliced ½ inch thick	1 tablespoon Worcestershire
1 green bell pepper, seeded and diced	Tabasco
1 stalk celery, chopped	3 cups shucked oysters and their liquor
	6 cups cooked white rice

Make a roux by heating the oil in a large heavy-bottomed pot over high heat. Whisk the flour into the hot oil. It will immediately begin to sizzle. Reduce the heat to medium and continue whisking until the roux turns a deep brown color, about 15 minutes. Add the onions, stirring them into the roux with a wooden spoon. Lower the heat to medium low and continue stirring until the roux turns a glossy dark brown, about 10 minutes.

Season the duck well with salt and pepper. Add the duck pieces to the pot, increase the heat to medium, and brown, turning the pieces, for about 10 minutes. Add the smoked sausage and stir for 1 minute or two; add the bell pepper, celery, and garlic. Cook, stirring, about 3 minutes more. Add the green onions, chicken stock, and bay leaves. Bring the gumbo to a boil, stirring occasionally. Reduce the heat to medium low and simmer for 45 minutes. Stir occasionally and skim off the fat from the surface of the gumbo (moving the pot half off the burner helps collect the impurities).

Add the andouille sausage and Worcestershire and season with Tabasco, salt, and pepper. Simmer for another 45 minutes, continuing to skim fat from the surface. Just before serving, add the oysters and their liquor. Serve the gumbo in bowls with rice.

GUMBO

What to do with all that leftover turkey was a perennial problem around our house. I solved that years ago with this gumbo, which adds such new flavor to the Thanksgiving bird that it doesn't seem like leftovers at all.

Day-After-Thanksgiving Turkey Gumbo

✦ Serves 10

¾ cup canola oil
¾ cup flour
1 onion, chopped
1 stalk celery, chopped
½ bell pepper, seeded and chopped
4 cloves garlic, minced
2 bay leaves
3 quarts Go-To Chicken Stock (page 27)

Meat picked from leftover roast turkey, plus the turkey carcass
2 pounds smoked sausage, sliced ½ inch thick
1 pound okra, sliced
Tabasco
Salt and pepper
6 cups cooked white rice
2 green onions, chopped

Make a roux by heating the oil in a large heavy-bottomed pot over high heat. Whisk the flour into the hot oil. It will immediately begin to sizzle. Reduce the heat to medium and continue whisking until the roux turns a deep brown color, about 15 minutes. Add the onions, stirring them into the roux with a wooden spoon. Lower the heat to medium low and continue stirring until the roux turns a glossy dark brown, about 10 minutes.

Add the celery, bell pepper, garlic, and bay leaves and stir for 3 minutes, then add the stock. Raise the heat to high and bring to a boil. Add the turkey carcass, sausage, and okra. Lower the heat and simmer for 45 minutes. Stir occasionally and skim the fat from the surface of the gumbo (moving the pot half off the burner helps collect the impurities). Remove the carcass from the pot.

Add the turkey meat and season well with Tabasco, salt, and pepper. Serve in bowls with rice, scattered with the green onions.

GUMBO

We New Orleanians are superstitious folk and it's said that for every different green you use in Gumbo z'Herbes (from the French *gumbo aux herbes*), you'll gain a new friend in the upcoming year. You can be sure we use every green we can get our hands on! Mustard, turnip, collard, kale, arugula, spinach, watercress, sorrel, even beet or carrot tops are all contenders. Some folks make it without meat, but I love the way the ham hocks flavor the greens.

Gumbo z'Herbes

✦ Serves 8

1	tablespoon bacon fat or oil	
3	onions, chopped	
1	stalk celery, chopped	
2	green onions, chopped	
4	cloves garlic, minced	
4	smoked ham hocks	
3	pounds greens, well washed and roughly chopped	
1	pound okra, sliced	

1	bay leaf
1	teaspoon dried thyme
1	clove, crushed
	Big pinch allspice
	Big pinch cayenne pepper
	Salt and pepper
4	cups cooked white rice

Heat the fat in a large heavy-bottomed pot over high heat and cook the onions, stirring, until they become translucent. Add the celery, green onions, and garlic and cook until soft. Add the ham hocks, greens, and water to cover. Cover the pot and bring to a boil. Lower the heat to a simmer and add the okra, bay leaf, thyme, clove, allspice, cayenne pepper, and a dash of salt. Cover the pot and cook slowly for about 2 hours.

Remove the pot from the heat and season with salt and pepper. Carefully remove the ham hocks and separate the meat from the bones. Discard the bones and chop the meat.

Remove the bay leaf and puree the soup in a blender; you may have to do this in batches. Serve the gumbo with rice and chunks of ham hock.

VEGGIES

❝ The Creole tomatoes of my childhood were ugly and deformed, split to the point of bursting. Today, Creole tomatoes have become self-conscious; they're just a little too smooth for me. We now have farmers who grow wonderfully sweet, sometimes even unattractive tomatoes in St. Tammany Parish on the North Shore of Lake Pontchartrain. So many of the vegetables I use at home come from Tara and Jack Collier's Camellia Produce in Slidell. ❞

Country Coleslaw

✦ Serves 6

❝ Cabbage is an obvious choice, but it's not the only vegetable for coleslaw. We make coleslaw with whatever vegetables and condiments happen to be in our refrigerator (hence the pickle relish). Variations are endless. This version is tangy and sweet, which makes it perfect with, well, almost anything. ❞

1 head cabbage, halved, cored, and thinly sliced	¼ cup shredded carrot
1 onion, thinly sliced	½ cup mayonnaise
2 green onions, chopped	½ cup rice wine vinegar
¼ cup sweet pickle relish	2 tablespoons sugar
	Salt and pepper

In a large serving bowl, mix together the cabbage, onions, green onions, pickle relish, and carrots. In another bowl, whisk together the mayonnaise, vinegar, sugar, salt, and pepper until well incorporated. Pour the dressing over the cabbage mixture and toss to coat well. Cover and refrigerate for an hour or so before serving.

❝ When tomatoes are so ripe you can smell their sweetness, that's the time to make these stuffed tomatoes. I love the contrast of the crunchy bread crumb topping with the lush, warm tomatoes. ❞

❝ I freeze countless containers of this barely cooked sauce for that inevitable moment when I need a hit of real tomatoes in a gumbo or a stew. It's like money in the bank. ❞

Stuffed Heirloom Tomatoes

✦ Serves 6-8

6 medium or large tomatoes	¼ cup grated Parmesan cheese
Salt and pepper	2 cloves garlic, peeled
½ cup olive oil	3 sprigs basil
½ cup dried bread crumbs	

Preheat the oven to 350°. Cut the tomatoes in half horizontally. Place in a baking pan, cut side up, and season generously with salt and pepper. Drizzle with 2 tablespoons of the olive oil.

In a blender, combine the remaining olive oil, the bread crumbs, Parmesan, garlic, basil, and 2 pinches of salt and process for about 1 minute. The mixture should have a wet, crumbly consistency.

Press the bread crumb mixture onto the tomato halves. Bake for 15 minutes, or until the tops are crispy brown and the tomatoes are warmed through.

Cherry Tomato Five-Minute Sauce

✦ Makes 6 cups

¼ cup olive oil	4 cloves garlic, crushed
2 quarts ripe cherry tomatoes, halved	Handful basil leaves
2 tablespoons crushed red pepper flakes	Salt and pepper

Heat the oil in a large saucepan over high heat. Add the tomatoes, pepper flakes, garlic, and basil and bring to a boil. Reduce the heat to medium and cook for another 5 minutes, stirring occasionally with a wooden spoon.

Pour the sauce into a food mill and puree. Season with salt and pepper. Transfer to quart containers and store in the freezer.

❝ This is a salad for folks who think they don't like eggplant. I love the contrast between the eggplant's crispy exterior and creamy insides. The fried eggplant is set off by ripe tomatoes and peppers, all held together by a sherry vinaigrette. ❞

Fried Eggplant Salad

✦ Serves 6

Olive oil
2 eggs
1 cup dried Italian bread crumbs
1 large eggplant, peeled and cut into small cubes
Salt
¼ cup sherry vinegar
1 teaspoon sugar

Salt and pepper
2 large handfuls mixed greens
4 small peppers of many colors, cored, seeded, and thinly sliced
2 cups cherry tomatoes, halved
Parmesan cheese, for shaving

Heat 3 inches of oil in a saucepan to 350°. Set out two shallow bowls. Beat the eggs in one and put the bread crumbs in the other. Dip the eggplant cubes first into the eggs, then into the bread crumbs, coating well.

Working in batches, drop the battered eggplant cubes into the oil and fry until golden brown on all sides, about 5 minutes. Drain on paper towels and salt well.

For the vinaigrette, mix together ¾ cup olive oil, the vinegar, sugar, salt, and pepper until well blended. Spoon the vinaigrette onto a serving platter. Top with the fried eggplant, greens, peppers, and tomatoes. Season with salt and pepper. Shave some Parmesan over the top and serve.

❝ Whenever I can serve mashed turnips instead of mashed potatoes, I leap at the chance. The lovely surprise of the mild turnip flavor complements so many meats and poultry: think duck, rabbit, pheasant, even chicken. ❞

❝ These chips are so addictive, it's hard to believe they're actually pretty good for you. As the chips fry, they'll need your close attention. Keep them moving in the pan with a slotted spoon, turning them often so they brown uniformly. ❞

Creamy Turnips

✦ Serves 6

4 purple turnips, peeled and quartered	1 sprig rosemary, optional
1 large Yukon Gold potato, peeled and quartered	4 tablespoons butter
Salt	Pepper

Put the turnips and potatoes in a medium saucepan, cover with water, and add salt and the rosemary sprig. Bring to a boil over high heat. Reduce the heat and simmer until tender, 20–25 minutes. Drain and discard the rosemary.

Combine the turnips, potatoes, and butter in a food processor and process into a smooth puree (or mash with a potato masher). Season with salt and pepper and serve.

Pan-Fried Sweet Potatoes

✦ Serves 8

2 cups canola oil	1 teaspoon ancho chili powder
4 sweet potatoes, peeled and cut into ¼-inch-thick slices	Salt

Heat the oil in a cast iron pan over medium heat until really hot. Add the potato slices in batches and pan-fry, turning often. Let them take their time so they're tender in the middle and crispy on the outside. Drain on paper towels, toss with the chili powder, and salt well.

Grilling okra seems to me an excellent idea, especially for those who don't love its natural gelatinous qualities. (I happen to prize okra for just that tendency to break down and make my gumbos silky.) For these grilled okra, I use the smallest, greenest pods I can find.

Grilled Okra

✦ Serves 4

1 pound okra	2 tablespoons freshly grated Parmesan cheese
¼ cup olive oil	Zest of 1 lemon
1 teaspoon salt	
1 teaspoon black pepper	

Toss the okra with the oil, salt, and pepper in a small bowl. Heat a gas or charcoal grill to hot (or use your oven's broiler). Grill the okra over a hot fire for 3–5 minutes, turning on all sides.

Remove to a serving bowl and toss with the Parmesan and lemon zest before serving.

❝ I love to use beets in a range of colors to enliven this salad. I prefer small beets because they are so tender, but if you use larger ones, please lower the oven temperature to 350° and let them roast longer—say, an hour. Peel, then cube and toss with the other ingredients. ❞

Roasted Beet Salad

✦ Serves 6

2 pounds small red and yellow beets	½ cup rice wine vinegar
½ cup olive oil	2 tablespoons sugar
Salt	Pepper
1 medium red onion, thinly sliced	

Preheat the oven to 425°. Rub the beets all over with half of the oil and then salt generously. Place on a baking sheet and roast until soft all the way through, about 25 minutes.

When the beets are cool enough to handle, peel and quarter them. Transfer to a bowl and toss with the remaining ¼ cup oil, the red onion, vinegar, and sugar. Season with more salt and pepper.

Roasted Brussels Sprout Salad

 This is such a simple idea that unfailingly gets great reviews from the dinner table. The idea is to toss the still-warm sprouts with a fragrant vinaigrette. You can serve them either warm or cold. 🙶

✦ Serves 6

1½ pounds Brussels sprouts, trimmed and halved

    Olive oil

    Salt and pepper

2 cloves garlic, sliced

2 tablespoons sherry vinegar

2 tablespoons sesame oil

2 tablespoons olive or walnut oil

Preheat the oven to 450°. Toss the Brussels sprouts in a baking pan with a generous amount of olive oil and season well with salt and pepper. Roast for about 20 minutes, until the sprouts are golden brown and tender, tossing occasionally.

Transfer to a large serving bowl and, while the sprouts are still hot, add the garlic, vinegar, and oils. Toss well, add more salt and pepper, and serve.

> Don't be afraid to mix this salad with your hands to distribute the vinaigrette and help saturate the tender cukes with all that lovely flavor.

Cucumber & White Onion Salad

✦ Serves 6

1 clove garlic, minced
2 tablespoons red wine vinegar
2 tablespoons olive oil
  Salt and pepper
  Red pepper flakes

4 Persian cucumbers, peeled and cubed
½ small white onion, thinly sliced
  Handful basil and parsley leaves, chopped

For the vinaigrette, whisk together the garlic, vinegar, and oil in a small bowl. Add salt, pepper, and a pinch of pepper flakes.

Combine the cucumbers, onions, basil, and parsley in a large bowl. Season with salt, pepper, and pepper flakes. Add the vinaigrette, toss, and let the flavors marinate for 30 minutes before serving.

> Whenever we're lucky enough to have a crawfish boil, one of the added benefits is the potato salad that we make the next day from the small red potatoes that were boiled in all those delicious spices. If you're lucky, you'll find a half head of garlic in there, too, to squeeze into the dressing.

Crawfish-Boil Potato Salad

✦ Serves 6-8

2 pounds Red Bliss potatoes, left over from a crawfish boil, quartered	2 green onions, diced
½ head garlic from crawfish boil, optional	1 cup mayonnaise
½ onion, diced	2 tablespoons Creole mustard
1 stalk celery, diced	1 teaspoon from My Jar of Creole Spices (page xi)
	Salt

Put the potatoes in a large mixing bowl. Squeeze the reserved garlic (if you have it) into the bowl. Add the onions, celery, green onions, mayonnaise, mustard, and spices. Season with salt and toss well.

VARIATION

Crawfish-Boil Home Fries

Red Bliss potatoes are our favorites to use in crawfish, crab, or shrimp boils. They're too deliciously seasoned not to fry them up again for breakfast. Just cook the potatoes in plenty of bacon fat in a large cast iron skillet until they're golden brown. Transfer to a platter, sprinkle green onions on top, and serve. What's not to like?

Jenny's Potato Salad

> 66 Sometimes great marriages happen in the kitchen. Such was the case when we introduced my egg salad to my wife's potato salad. A match made in heaven! 99

✦ Serves 8-10

3	pounds Yukon Gold potatoes	1	onion, minced
8	eggs	1	stalk celery, minced
1¼	cups mayonnaise	3	green onions, chopped
¼	cup white wine vinegar	1	clove garlic, minced
¼	cup sweet pickle relish		Salt and pepper
2	tablespoons Creole mustard		

Put the potatoes in a large heavy-bottomed pot and add salted water to cover by 2 inches. Bring to a boil, then reduce to a simmer and cook until the potatoes are fork tender, about 30 minutes. Drain and cool. When the potatoes are cool enough to handle, use a small knife to remove the skin. Roughly chop the potatoes into large chunks.

While the potatoes are cooking, put the eggs in a saucepan, cover with water, and bring to a boil over high heat. Cover the pan and immediately remove from the heat. Let the eggs sit in the hot water for 5-7 minutes. Place the pot in the sink under the faucet and let cold water run until the eggs have cooled enough to handle. Peel and roughly chop the eggs.

For the dressing, whisk together the mayonnaise, vinegar, relish, and mustard in a small bowl until well combined. Add the onions, celery, green onions, and garlic and stir well.

Combine the potatoes and eggs in a large serving bowl. Add the dressing and toss to combine. Season with salt and pepper and refrigerate until ready to serve.

" The dream sandwich of my childhood was thick slices of Creole tomatoes on white Bunny bread slathered with our Blue Plate mayonnaise. "

SHRIMP, CRAB & CRAWFISH

❝ As kids we'd eat shrimp creole over white rice, sautéed jumbo shrimp with pasta, shrimp remoulade, and shrimp cocktail which Mom would serve in little cups nestled in crushed ice. Our shrimp often came from generous friends. When we did buy it, we'd get a hundred pounds or so, which meant a long night ahead for Mom and me, peeling shrimp and freezing them in containers made from cut off milk jugs. ❞

Growing up, we'd go to these little joints all around New Orleans that had great stuffed shrimp. But the dish has changed so much. Now it's all premade, pre-stuffed, and fried. I still make stuffed shrimp the way I remember them. I love the presentation: head-on jumbo shrimp are stuffed with more shrimp and crabmeat piled as high as the shrimp will allow.

Stuffed Jumbo Shrimp

✦ Serves 6

- 2 tablespoons butter
- 1 shallot, minced
- 3 cloves garlic, minced
- 1 stalk celery, minced
- 2 tablespoons flour
- ½ pound medium wild American shrimp, peeled, deveined, and chopped
- ½ pound crabmeat
- 1 green onion, minced
- ½ cup Shrimp Stock (page 27) or water

- ½ cup fresh bread crumbs
- 1 teaspoon crushed red pepper flakes
  Salt and pepper
- ½ cup dried bread crumbs
- ½ cup grated Parmesan cheese
- ½ cup olive oil
- 1 teaspoon fresh thyme
- 18 jumbo wild American shrimp, peeled with heads and tails on

Preheat the oven to 425°. Melt the butter in a medium skillet over medium-high heat. Add the shallots, garlic, and celery and cook, stirring often, until the vegetables are soft, about 5 minutes. Sprinkle the flour into the skillet and stir until mixed into the vegetables. You're making a blond roux. Add the chopped medium shrimp, crabmeat, and green onion. Slowly add the stock, stirring until sauce thickens; remove from the heat. Add the fresh bread crumbs, pepper flakes, salt, and pepper. Set the stuffing aside.

Mix together the dried bread crumbs, Parmesan, oil, and thyme in a small bowl until the oil moistens the mixture. Set the topping aside.

With a small knife, butterfly the jumbo shrimp by making a deep incision down the back of each. Remove the vein, keeping the head and tail intact. Smear some olive oil all over the shrimp with your hands. Salt and pepper well and transfer to a baking pan, open side up.

Generously fill each jumbo shrimp with stuffing and top with the bread crumb topping. Bake until golden, 12–15 minutes.

❝ Even if she wasn't my mother-in-law, I'd be happy eating Barbara Berrigan's creamy and elegant shrimp salad every day! Take the time to finely chop all the ingredients; it makes all the difference in the texture of the salad. ❞

Barbara's Shrimp Salad

✦ Serves 6

1 pound boiled wild American shrimp, deveined and finely chopped

½ stalk celery, minced

2 green onions, finely chopped

2 hard-boiled eggs, minced

¾ cup mayonnaise

1 tablespoon Creole mustard

1 tablespoon prepared horseradish

4 dashes Tabasco

½ teaspoon from My Creole Spice Jar (page xi) or 1 teaspoon Zatarain's Shrimp & Crab Boil

Mix all the ingredients together in a large bowl, and season with more Tabasco or more spices as needed. I like to serve the salad with toasts, or in a sandwich, or the way Miss Barbara does—stuffed into a fresh tomato half for lunch.

New Orleans Shrimp Étouffée

✦ Serves 4-6

¼ cup canola oil
¼ cup flour
1 onion, chopped
1 stalk celery, chopped
4 cloves garlic, minced
  Pinch allspice
  Pinch cayenne pepper
½ cup chopped tomatoes
2½ cups Shellfish Stock (page 27)

3 tablespoons butter
1 pound medium wild American shrimp, peeled and deveined
1 green onion, minced
  Tabasco
  Salt and pepper
4 cups cooked white rice

Make a roux by heating the oil in a large heavy-bottomed pot over high heat. Whisk the flour into the hot oil. It will immediately begin to sizzle. Reduce the heat to medium and continue whisking until the roux turns a deep brown color, about 15 minutes. Add the onions, stirring them into the roux with a wooden spoon. Lower the heat to medium low and continue stirring until the roux turns a glossy dark brown, about 10 minutes.

When the onions have turned the roux shiny and dark, add the celery, garlic, allspice, and cayenne. Cook for 5 minutes. Then add the tomatoes and stock and raise the heat to high. Once the sauce has come to a boil, lower the heat to medium and simmer 5–7 minutes, stirring often to make sure the sauce doesn't burn or stick to the pan.

Reduce the heat to low and stir in the butter. Add the shrimp and green onions. Season with Tabasco, salt, and pepper. Once the shrimp are heated through, remove the pot from the heat. Serve over rice.

This succulent 'smothered' stew is often made with crawfish or crab instead of shrimp. Just make sure to add the shrimp at the end, so they stay plump and juicy. Making étouffée is all about building flavor: starting with a velvety roux, cooking the vegetables longer than you'd think, and scraping all those tasty bits off the bottom of the pan with a wooden spoon. The sauce should be only thick enough to coat the rice.

SHRIMP, CRAB & CRAWFISH

❝ There are fancier ways to make classic New Orleans 'barbecue' shrimp, but why make it more complicated than it needs to be? This shrimp is not even barbecued. Instead, whole, fat shrimp are drowned in butter, lots of black pepper, and beer. The deep flavor comes from toasting the shrimp in their shells in a baking pan to hold the abundant sauce which is as good as the shrimp. ❞

Quick & Dirty BBQ Shrimp

✦ Serves 6

2 pounds large wild American shrimp, heads and shells on

1 tablespoon olive oil

6 tablespoons black peppercorns, crushed

6 cloves garlic, sliced

1 bottle beer

¼ cup Worcestershire

1 branch fresh rosemary or 1 teaspoon dried rosemary

Juice of 1 lemon

10 tablespoons butter

Salt

Lay the shrimp in a roasting pan and top with all the remaining ingredients. Stir the sauce over high heat until the butter has melted. Lower the heat and simmer for a few minutes, until the shrimp turn pink all over. Serve with plenty of French bread for sopping up that great sauce.

❝ Crabs shed their shells some 20 times in their lifetime, but our soft shell crab season is a short one. Ask your fishmonger to help find soft shell crabs. ❞

❝ This dressing is so good, you could use it to stuff almost anything: large mushrooms, halved winter squash or mirlitons, even a chicken. You could easily substitute shrimp for the crawfish. ❞

Crawfish-Stuffed Soft Shell Crabs

✦ Serves 4

Canola oil for frying	2 cups cornmeal
4 soft shell crabs, cleaned	Big pinch dried thyme
Crawfish Dressing (recipe follows)	Big pinch cayenne pepper
2 cups buttermilk	Salt and pepper
	Lemon wedges for serving

Heat ½ inch oil in a cast iron pan or heavy skillet to 350°. With a small knife, create a pocket under the top shell of each crab and stuff with the crawfish dressing. Set out two shallow bowls, one with the buttermilk, the other with the cornmeal mixed with the thyme, cayenne, salt, and pepper. Dip the crabs first in the buttermilk and then the cornmeal mixture.

Fry the stuffed crabs until they are golden brown on both sides, turning carefully with a spatula. Remove the crabs and drain on paper towels. Serve immediately with lemon wedges.

CRAWFISH DRESSING

✦ Makes 2 cups

4 tablespoons butter	2 eggs
3 green onions, chopped	¾ cup dried Italian bread crumbs
3 cloves garlic, sliced	Pinch cayenne pepper
½ pound shelled crawfish tails, chopped	Salt and pepper

Melt the butter in a skillet over medium-high heat, add the green onions, garlic, and crawfish, and cook for 2–3 minutes. Spoon into a mixing bowl, add the eggs, bread crumbs, cayenne, salt, and pepper and stir to combine.

> "Everything is overstuffed down here. Mr. Sam's Crabs have plenty of fresh bread crumbs in the stuffing, and lots of dried crumbs to make the topping crispy."

❝ Crabs are to New Orleans what caviar is to the Black Sea. The mom-and-pop places I knew as a young cook influenced me far more than any of the city's famous, fancy restaurants. I learned these stuffed crabs from Mr. Sam Manascalco, who owned the Cast Net, the first restaurant I worked at. I like to use shells left over from a crab boil, keeping all that good juice. ❞

Mr. Sam's Stuffed Crabs

✦ Serves 6

1 pound crabmeat	Big pinch allspice
1 onion, minced	Salt
1 green onion, minced	6 blue crab top shells
4 cloves garlic, thinly sliced	¼ cup dried bread crumbs
½ cup mayonnaise	¼ cup grated Parmesan cheese
½ cup fresh bread crumbs	¼ cup olive oil
1 teaspoon dried tarragon	
1 teaspoon crushed red pepper flakes	

Preheat the oven to 400°. In a large mixing bowl, combine the crabmeat with the onions, green onions, garlic, mayonnaise, fresh bread crumbs, tarragon, pepper flakes, allspice, and salt. Toss and taste to see if it needs a bit more spice, then generously stuff the crab shells and put in a baking pan.

In another bowl, mix the dried bread crumbs, Parmesan, and oil until the oil moistens the mixture. Sprinkle this topping over each crab. Bake for 12–16 minutes, until the crabs are golden brown and hot in the middle.

RICE, BEANS & CORN

> **"** Come summer, as crawfish burrow into the swampy Louisiana lowland, long grain rice begins to flourish. It's glorious to gaze out over miles of those once-watery fields and see tall rice stalks rippling like wheat in the breeze. After the rice is harvested in late summer, a second crop often emerges. Since this second crop is relatively low yield it's usually left in the field to feed wintering waterfowl as well as the next generation of crawfish. Now that's what I consider a magical circle of life. **"**

It's a tradition in NOLA to eat red beans and rice on Monday. Here's my Big Easy way to cook rice: Put a couple of tablespoons chicken fat, oil, or butter in a saucepan; add some chopped onion; sweat it down; then add a bay leaf and a pinch of salt. Soften the onions, add the rice, and stir to coat until the grains are shiny. Add stock or water: 2 parts liquid to 1 part rice. Stir, cover, and simmer for 20 minutes.

Monday's Red Beans & Rice

✦ Serves 6

2 tablespoons bacon fat or oil	1 smoked ham hock
1 onion, chopped	3 bay leaves
½ green bell pepper, seeded and chopped	Salt and pepper
1 stalk celery, chopped	Tabasco
1 pound dried red kidney beans, soaked in water overnight and drained	4-6 cups cooked white rice
	2 green onions, chopped

Heat the bacon fat in a large heavy-bottomed pot over medium-high heat and sweat the onions, bell peppers, and celery. Once the onions become translucent, add the beans, ham hock, bay leaves, and water to cover by 2 inches. Raise the heat, bring the water to a boil, then lower the heat and cover the pot. Let the beans slowly simmer for 2 hours, stirring from time to time to make sure they do not stick and adding water to keep them covered by at least an inch. Continue cooking the beans until they become so tender they begin to fall apart and become creamy when stirred.

Remove the ham hock from the pot and take the meat off the bone. Roughly chop and return to the pot. Season with salt, pepper, and Tabasco. Serve the beans in bowls topped with white rice and green onions.

❝❝ Think of this as Creole fried rice. Cooked rice (can be leftovers) is stirred up with browned sausage, onions, and chicken livers (which is where the dish got its name). I like to make Dirty Rice and use it to stuff a chicken; imagine how good that is! ❞❞

❝❝ This is just a fancy version of Dirty Rice. Made with crabmeat, fresh green peas, and any wild mushrooms you can get your hands on, it can be a meal in itself. ❞❞

Dirty Rice

✦ Serves 8

2 tablespoons bacon fat or oil
1 pound fresh pork sausage, removed from casings
1 onion, chopped
1 stalk celery, chopped
4 cloves garlic, minced
½ pound chicken livers, chopped
1 teaspoon crushed red pepper flakes

1 teaspoon dried sage
1 cup Go-To Chicken Stock (page 27) or water
8 cups cooked white rice
2 green onions, chopped
Tabasco
Worcestershire
Salt and pepper

Heat the bacon fat in a large heavy skillet over medium-high heat. Add the sausage and cook until well browned. Add the onions, celery, and garlic and cook until they are caramelized, about 10 minutes. Add the livers, pepper flakes, sage, and stock and heat through. Stir in the rice, green onions, Tabasco, Worcestershire, salt, and pepper. Serve as is or use as stuffing.

Crab & Sausage Fried Rice

✦ Serves 8

¼ cup olive oil
Big handful wild mushrooms, chopped
Salt and pepper
1 pound smoked sausage, chopped
2 cloves garlic, thinly sliced

2-3 cups cooked rice
1 cup green peas, fresh or frozen
1 pound crabmeat
2 green onions, chopped
Tabasco

Heat the oil in a large skillet over high heat. Add the wild mushrooms and cook until browned. Add salt and pepper. Lower the heat to medium-high and add the smoked sausage. Then add the garlic and sweat until translucent. Stir in the rice, then the green peas and crabmeat and stir just until warmed through. Stir in the green onions and season with Tabasco and more salt and pepper.

In New Orleans, we're fairly superstitious. We have to have our black-eyed peas with New Year's Dinner. We also like creamy beans, we like creamy peas, we like creamy everything! We can get so many different kinds of field peas: black-eyed peas, crowder peas, purple hull peas. We cook them fresh in season; but dried is the next best thing. They take longer to cook, but taste wonderful—creamy peas in their flavorful cooking juices.

Field Peas in Pot Liquor

✦ Serves 8

2 tablespoons bacon fat or oil
1 medium onion, chopped
1 clove garlic, crushed
1 smoked ham hock
1 bay leaf

Pinch crushed red pepper flakes
1 pound fresh field peas, or dried peas, soaked in water overnight

Heat the bacon fat in a large heavy-bottomed pot over medium-high heat. Add the onions and garlic and cook until soft, about 5 minutes. Add the ham hock, bay leaf, pepper flakes, field peas, and water to cover by 2 inches. Cover the pot, bring to a boil, then lower the heat to a simmer. Cook for 45 minutes to 1 hour, adding more water if needed, until the peas are tender. Remove the ham hock and serve the meat with the peas if you like.

Sweet Corn Macque Choux

✦ Serves 6-8

❝❞ This classic Cajun dish of corn stewed in cream has Native American roots, but no connection whatsoever to the French word for cabbage, *choux.* I like to make it when our corn is at peak ripeness, for the sweet corn flavor is what macque choux is all about. I usually serve it straight from the pan as soon as the tomatoes begin to soften into the creamy corn. ❞❞

6 ears sweet corn, kernels sliced off the cob	½ serrano pepper, thinly sliced
1 onion, chopped	1 cup cherry tomatoes, halved
2 tablespoons butter	1 cup heavy cream
2 cloves garlic, minced	Salt and pepper

Cook the corn and onions in the buuter in a large skillet over medium heat until they are soft and translucent. Add the garlic and serrano and cook a few minutes longer. Add the tomatoes and cream, raise the heat, and bring to a boil. Lower the heat and simmer for a few minutes. Add salt and pepper and serve.

❝ For years, I've used Frank McEwen's organic stone ground corn products: cornmeal, polenta, and white, yellow, blue, and speckled grits. The quality that comes from his Alabama mill (mcewenandsons.com) is consistently outstanding. ❞

Baked Cheesy Grits

✦ Serves 6

1 tablespoon salt	1 cup grated provolone or mozzarella cheese
4 tablespoons butter	½ cup cream cheese
1 cup stone ground grits	Pinch red pepper flakes

Bring 1 quart water, the salt, and butter to a boil in a large saucepan, then slowly whisk in the grits. Lower the heat and cook, stirring often, until the grits become soft and creamy, about 20 minutes. Remove from the heat and fold in the cheeses, pepper flakes, and more salt. Serve right from the pan, or transfer to a skillet and bake at 350° for 15 minutes.

Silver Queen Corn Pudding

How can a pudding be so silky and elegant and yet so down-home comfortable? Make this one and you'll see.

✦ Serves 8

4 cups heavy cream	Salt
6 cups fresh corn kernels (from about 12 ears)	Big pinch cayenne pepper
10 eggs, beaten	Butter for the baking dish
1 teaspoon sugar	

Preheat the oven to 325°. Bring the cream and corn to a boil in a large saucepan. Reduce the heat and simmer for 5 minutes.

Pour the corn and cream into a blender and puree, slowly adding the eggs while blending. Add the sugar, salt, and cayenne pepper and pour the corn puree into a large buttered baking dish. Bake for about 20 minutes, until golden brown and puffed. Let the pudding rest a few minutes before serving.

❝ Your friends are going to love me for teaching you this recipe. What's not to like about these hot, crispy balls of corn and crab in a cornmeal batter? It's like hush puppies married to crab cakes. ❞

Corn & Crab Fritters

✦ Serves 10–12

	Canola oil, for frying	1	pound crabmeat
8	tablespoons butter	1	cup stone ground cornmeal
1	cup corn kernels (from about 2 ears)	½	cup flour
2	eggs, beaten	1½	tablespoons baking powder
1	cup sour cream	1	tablespoon sugar
3	green onions, chopped	2	teaspoons salt
1	jalapeño pepper, seeded and minced	½	teaspoon ground pepper

Heat about 3 inches oil in a small saucepan to 350°. Melt the butter and pour into a mixing bowl. Stir in the corn, eggs, sour cream, green onions, and jalapeño. Fold in the crabmeat.

In another bowl, mix together the cornmeal, flour, baking powder, sugar, salt, and pepper. Stir the dry ingredients into the crabmeat mixture until well combined.

Wet your hands and form small balls of the fritter mixture. Drop, a few at a time, into the hot oil and fry for 3–4 minutes, turning, until the fritters are brown on all sides. Transfer to paper towels to drain and sprinkle with salt. Serve immediately.

Grandaddy's Skillet Corn Bread

✦ Makes 1 pone

🏠🏠 My Grandaddy Walters made the corn bread in our family and never the same way twice. He wouldn't give out the recipe, but I watched him and pretty much figured it out. He made sure to get his seasoned cast iron skillet so hot that the batter began to fry the second it hit the pan. That's the secret of the crispiest crust. 🗨🗨

3 tablespoons bacon fat or oil	2 tablespoons baking powder
1 cup stone ground cornmeal	1 teaspoon salt
1 cup flour	2 eggs
2 tablespoons sugar	1¼ cups milk
	2 tablespoons butter, melted

Preheat the oven to 425°. Put the bacon fat into a seasoned cast iron skillet and slide the skillet into the oven to heat for a few minutes.

Stir together the cornmeal, flour, sugar, baking powder, and salt in a large mixing bowl. In another bowl, mix the eggs, milk, and melted butter. Pour the egg mixture into the cornmeal mixture, stirring until just combined.

Carefully remove the hot skillet from the oven. Pour the batter into the skillet and watch it bubble up. Return the skillet to the oven and bake until the corn bread is deep golden brown, 15–20 minutes.

JAMBALAYA

There are many theories about the origination of the rice-based jambalaya. I've always heard that the word had Provençal roots from *jambon*, French for ham. And *ya* is African for rice. But since the Spanish town of Gonzales, Louisiana, calls itself the official 'Jambalaya Capital of the World' with a festival every spring, and even a Jambalaya Queen, I believe our jambalaya to be closer to the Spanish paella.

🔊 Make sure you're careful about adding the ingredients to the pot in the right order and at the correct time.

It's really important to begin the process of making this dish by browning the pork, sausage, and onions, which add both color and depth of flavor to the jambalaya. 🔊🔊

Pork Shoulder & Country Sausage Brown Jambalaya

✦ Serves 8-10

2 tablespoons canola oil	4 cups white rice
½ pound bacon, chopped	1 teaspoon dried thyme
1 pound pork shoulder, chopped	2 bay leaves
1 pound smoked pork sausage, sliced	1 teaspoon salt
1 pound fresh spicy sausage, casings removed	1 teaspoon black pepper
1 large onion, chopped	2 cups canned crushed tomatoes
1 bell pepper, seeded and chopped	6 cups Go-To Chicken Stock (page 27)
1 stalk celery, with leaves, chopped	Big pinch crushed red pepper flakes
4 cloves garlic, minced	4 green onions, chopped

Heat a very big, heavy-bottomed pot over high heat, then reduce the heat to medium. (This lets the pot heat uniformly, preventing hot spots which are likely to burn.) Add the oil, then the bacon, pork shoulder, sausage, and sausage meat and brown well, stirring slowly with a long wooden spoon to build color.

Add the onions and let them caramelize for about 15 minutes to build more flavor. I add the bell peppers late, to save as much of the color as I can. Add the celery (I always use the leaves, too) and garlic, and cook for about 5 minutes, stirring occasionally so that everything cooks evenly.

Next add the rice, thyme, bay leaves, salt, and pepper to the pot and cook, stirring often, for about 3 minutes. Increase the heat to high and add the tomatoes, stock, and pepper flakes. Bring the liquid to a boil, then reduce the heat to medium low, cover, and simmer for 15 minutes.

After the rice has simmered for 15 minutes, fold in the green onions. Cover again, turn off the heat, and let the rice continue to steam in the hot pot for another 10 minutes. Fluff the jambalaya with a fork and serve!

Live music breaks out anywhere in New Orleans, like this pickup band in the French Market, or almost anytime day or night on Frenchmen Street.

JAMBALAYA

Creole Seafood Jambalaya

✦ Serves 6

½ pound andouille or other smoked sausage, chopped

1 pound fresh pork sausage, removed from casings

½ cup bacon fat or oil

1 large onion, chopped

1 bell pepper, seeded and chopped

1 stalk celery, with leaves, chopped

3 garlic cloves, minced

2 cups white rice

1 teaspoon dried thyme

1 teaspoon cayenne pepper

2 bay leaves

1 cup crushed tomatoes

2 cups Go-To Chicken Stock (page 27)

1½ pounds medium wild American shrimp, peeled and deveined

Salt and pepper

2 green onions, chopped

Heat a very big, heavy-bottomed pot over high heat, then reduce the heat to medium. (This lets the pot heat uniformly, preventing hot spots which are likely to burn.) Brown the andouille and pork sausage in the bacon fat, stirring slowly with a long wooden spoon to build color.

After the sausages have browned, add the onions and let them caramelize for about 15 minutes to build more flavor. I add the bell peppers late, to save as much of the color as I can. Add the celery (I always use the leaves, too) and garlic, and cook for about 5 minutes, stirring occasionally so that everything cooks evenly.

Next add the rice, thyme, cayenne, and bay leaves to the pot and cook, stirring often, for about 3 minutes. Increase the heat to high and add the tomatoes and stock. Bring the liquid to a boil, then reduce the heat to medium low, cover, and simmer for 15 minutes.

While the rice is cooking, season the shrimp with salt and pepper. After the rice has simmered 15 minutes, fold in the shrimp and green onions. Cover again, turn off the heat, and let everything continue to cook in the hot pot for another 10 minutes. Fluff the jambalaya with a fork and serve!

This doesn't need to be too spicy. That's not what jambalaya is all about. It's not what New Orleans food is all about. It's about flavor, not spice. You can spice it up at the table.

Chicken & Andouille Jambalaya

✦ Serves 8-10

1 pound andouille or other smoked sausage, chopped	4 cloves garlic, minced
1 pound fresh pork sausage, removed from casings	4 cups white rice
½ cup bacon fat or oil	1 tablespoon pimentón (smoked paprika)
8 skinless boneless chicken thighs, roughly cut into cubes	1 teaspoon Cayenne pepper
Salt and pepper	1 teaspoon dried thyme
2 large onions, chopped	1 bay leaf
1 bell pepper, seeded and chopped	1 cup canned crushed tomatoes
1 stalk celery, with leaves, chopped	6 cups Go-To Chicken Stock (page 27)
	Big dash Tabasco
	Big dash Worcestershire
	4 green onions, chopped

Heat a very big, heavy-bottomed pot over high heat, then reduce the heat to medium. (This lets the pot heat uniformly, preventing hot spots that are likely to burn.) Brown the andouille and pork sausage in the bacon fat, stirring slowly with a long wooden spoon to build color. While the sausage is browning, season the chicken thighs with salt and pepper. Add the chicken to the pot (that dark meat is so flavorful!), stir, and cook until the chicken turns golden brown, about 5 minutes.

Once the chicken has browned, add the onions and let them caramelize for about 15 minutes to build more flavor. I add the bell peppers late, to save as much of the color as I can. Add the celery (I always use the leaves, too) and garlic and cook for about 5 minutes, stirring occasionally so that everything cooks evenly.

Next add the rice, pimentón, cayenne, thyme, bay leaf, 2 tablespoons salt, and 1 tablespoon pepper to the pot and cook, stirring often, for about 3 minutes. Increase the heat to high and add the tomatoes, stock, Tabasco, and Worcestershire. Bring the liquid to a boil, then reduce the heat to medium low, cover, and simmer for 15 minutes.

Fold in the green onions. Cover again, turn off the heat, and let the rice steam in the hot pot for another 10 minutes. Fluff the jambalaya with a fork and serve!

> **▲▲** The genius of jambalaya is that you can make it with just about any ingredients you have on hand, just as our ancestors did. If you're lucky enough to have some wild ducks from a good hunt, by all means use them. But any other small birds will work fine, too. I love our peppery, smoked pork shoulder butt called *tasso,* but any smoked pork will be great here. **▼▼**

Wild Duck & Tasso Jambalaya

✦ Serves 8–10

½	cup bacon fat or oil	4	cloves garlic, minced
1	pound tasso, chopped	4	cups white rice
1	pound fresh pork sausage, removed from casings	1	teaspoon dried thyme
4	wild ducks (about 2 pounds each), quartered	1	teaspoon cayenne pepper
		2	bay leaves
	Salt and pepper	1	cup canned crushed tomatoes
2	large onions, chopped	6	cups Go-To Chicken Stock (page 27)
1	bell pepper, seeded and chopped	4	green onions, chopped
1	stalk celery, with leaves, chopped		

Heat a very big, heavy-bottomed pot over high heat, then reduce the heat to medium. (This lets the pot heat uniformly, preventing hot spots which are likely to burn.) Add the bacon fat, tasso, and sausage and brown well, stirring slowly with a long wooden spoon to build color.

While the sausage is browning, season the ducks with salt and black pepper. Add the ducks to the pot, stirring, and cook until they become golden brown, about 5 minutes. Once the ducks have browned, add the onions and let them caramelize for about 15 minutes to build more flavor. I add the bell peppers late, to save as much of the color as I can. Add the celery (I always use the leaves, too) and garlic and cook for about 5 minutes, stirring occasionally so that everything cooks evenly.

Next add the rice, thyme, cayenne, and bay leaves to the pot and cook, stirring often, for about 3 minutes. Increase the heat to high and add the tomatoes and stock. Bring the liquid to a boil, then reduce the heat to medium low, cover, and simmer for 15 minutes.

After the rice has simmered for 15 minutes, fold in the green onions. Cover again, turn off the heat, and let the rice continue to steam in the hot pot for another 10 minutes. Fluff the jambalaya with a fork and serve!

BIG FISH

❝ People can be funny about cooking fish at home. They have a tendency to cook fish like meat. Wrong! Fish is delicate and subtle and cooking it must be too. Cooking fish properly starts with a first-rate fishmonger (like my great friend Brian Cappy, at Kenney's in Slidell) who will sell you the freshest fish and will skin, scale, and portion the fish for you. Hints: Cook small fish whole on the bone (that's where the flavor is); quickly sauté white flaky fish. As for meaty fish like salmon, tuna, and amberjack—they go on the grill. **❞**

BIG FISH

66 Everything tastes better with some Lake Pontchartrain crabmeat, and that's super true of this flounder. Every joint in New Orleans used to have stuffed flounder on the menu, and most were served on the bone. You can try to remove the bones, or just slit the fish down the middle, peel back the filets, and stuff the fish on the bone. This one's almost as good as my mamma's! Serve it with or without the sauce. 99

Crabmeat-Stuffed Flounder

✦ Serves 4-6

1 large flounder, scaled and gutted
½ onion, chopped
4 cloves garlic, thinly sliced
1 stalk celery, chopped
2 tablespoons olive oil
¼ cup Shellfish Stock (page 27) or water
½ pound crabmeat
Pinch crushed red pepper flakes

Salt and pepper
¼ cup diced white bread
¼ cup Italian dried bread crumbs
¾ cup Shellfish Pan Sauce (page 55)
Juice of 1 lemon
1 teaspoon Creole mustard
Big pinch dried thyme
2 tablespoons butter

Make a pocket for stuffing the flounder by carefully cutting from the gills to the tail along the backbone. Release the two filets with a flexible knife, making sure to leave some of the filet attached so you'll have a large pocket to stuff.

Preheat the oven to 400°. Cook the onions, garlic, and celery in the oil in a large skillet over medium heat, stirring until the vegetables are soft. Add the stock, crabmeat, and pepper flakes and cook for another 10 minutes, stirring. Add salt and pepper, then add the diced bread and bread crumbs and mix thoroughly. Stuff into the pocket of the flounder. Overstuffing is fine.

Drizzle with a bit more oil and place the fish in a lightly oiled baking pan. Cover the pan with foil and bake for 20 minutes.

Reduce the shellfish pan sauce by half in a small saucepan over medium-high heat. Add the lemon juice, mustard, and thyme. Remove from the heat, add the butter, and stir well.

Remove the foil from the flounder and return the pan to the oven for 5-7 minutes to crisp the stuffing. Serve with the sauce.

“ I just love our Louisiana crabmeat and maybe I'm guilty of adding it to any dish that will stand still long enough, but that's just the way things are done here. As my old Chef Chris used to say at La Provence, 'If you want to sell it, add a little crabmeat.' Any firm white-fleshed fish is great cooked this way. ”

Pan-Roasted Blackfish with Crab Butter

✦ Serves 4

- 4   5-ounce blackfish filets
  Salt and pepper
- ½   cup flour
- ¼   cup finely grated Parmesan cheese
- ¼   cup olive oil
- 8   tablespoons butter
- 1   cup halved cherry tomatoes
- 1   clove garlic, thinly sliced
- 1   green onion, chopped
- ½   serrano pepper, thinly sliced
  Juice of 1 lemon
- 1   pound crabmeat

Season the filets with salt and pepper. In a small bowl, mix together the flour and Parmesan and dredge the filets in the mixture.

Heat the oil in a large skillet over medium-high heat and sauté the fish until golden brown on both sides. Transfer the fish to a platter and keep warm for a few moments.

Add the butter to the skillet with the tomatoes, garlic, green onions, serrano peppers, and lemon juice. Cook for a few minutes and add the crabmeat, salt, and pepper. Lower the heat and cook until heated through. Spoon the crab butter over the filets and serve.

Lemonfish is big fish, native to the Gulf of Mexico. You can still see them out there following the shrimp boats. In other parts of the country, you can choose another meaty fish like mahi mahi or albacore tuna. I like to carve away the excess and just use the dense, flavorful loin.

Herb-Grilled Lemonfish Loin

✦ Serves 6-8

5 tablespoons olive oil

3 cloves garlic, crushed

1 teaspoon salt

1 teaspoon herbes de Provence

½ teaspoon crushed red pepper flakes

Zest and juice of 1 lemon

3 pounds lemonfish

Small handful each of fresh parsley and basil leaves, chopped

Salt and pepper

Heat a grill or broiler to high. Make a puree of 2 tablespoons of the oil, the garlic, salt, herbes de Provence, pepper flakes, and lemon zest in a food processor.

Rub the fish with the herb paste. Sear the fish on the grill or under the broiler for a few minutes on each side until the fish is cooked through. Remove to a platter.

In a small bowl, combine the remaining 3 tablespoons oil, the lemon juice, chopped herbs, salt, and pepper. Slice the fish against the grain and drizzle with the herb oil.

Mustard-Fried Catfish with Jalapeño Tartar Sauce

✦ Serves 6

Canola oil, for frying
6 catfish filets, boneless and skinless
Salt and pepper
¼ cup Creole mustard
8 dashes Tabasco

4 cups fine ground cornmeal
Jalapeño Tartar Sauce

Heat 3 inches of canola oil in a saucepan over medium-high until it reaches 350°.

Generously season the filets with salt and pepper. Set out two shallow bowls. Mix the mustard and Tabasco in one, and put the cornmeal in the other. Dip the filets first in the mustard/Tabasco mix then into the cornmeal. In batches,

BIG FISH

This is such a classic old-timer way to fry fish. They'd just make it with what they had. They wouldn't mess around with egg wash, just toss the catfish with Creole mustard and Tabasco, then straight into the cornmeal. The vinegar in the mustard makes an incredibly crispy crust. It's great with a simple chile tartar sauce.

gently slide the filets into the hot oil and fry for 3 minutes. Turn the pieces over with a slotted spoon and cook another 3 minutes. Drain on paper towels and season with more salt and pepper. Serve with the tartar sauce.

JALAPEÑO TARTAR SAUCE

✦ Makes about 1½ cups

1   cup mayonnaise
    Juice of 1 lemon
2   tablespoons white wine vinegar
1   tablespoon Creole mustard
2   green onions, chopped
1   jalapeño pepper, minced
    Salt and pepper

Mix all ingredients together in a small bowl.

The presentation of this whole roasted fish is such a knockout that I usually bring it to the table and serve it right from the pan, spooning the fish and vegetables onto each plate with plenty of delicious pan sauce.

Whole Roasted Snapper with Cherry Tomatoes

✦ Serves 4

1 large snapper, scaled and gutted	1 pint cherry tomatoes, halved
Salt and pepper	2 small red and yellow bell peppers, sliced
4 cloves garlic, smashed	½ cup pitted olives, black or green
1 shallot, sliced	
Big pinch crushed red pepper flakes	1 cup white wine
4 sprigs thyme	4 tablespoons butter
1 orange, sliced	2 green onions, chopped
3 tablespoons olive oil	Leaves from 2 sprigs basil
1 small fennel bulb, chopped	

Preheat the oven to 450°. Score the fish and season inside and out with salt and pepper. Stuff the fish with the garlic, shallots, pepper flakes, thyme, and orange slices. Spoon the oil into a roasting pan and lay the fish on top. Scatter the fennel, tomatoes, peppers, and olives all around. Add the wine.

Roast until the fish is white and flaky and the tomatoes are beautifully charred, about 20 minutes. Stir the butter into the pan and toss with the vegetables. Sprinkle the snapper with green onions and basil and serve right from the pan with the pan sauce.

Pan-Fried Puppy Drum with Crabmeat & Wild Mushrooms

✦ Serves 6

½ cup flour	1 handful wild mushrooms, sliced
1 tablespoon from My Jar of Creole Spices (page xi)	1 shallot, minced
2 eggs, beaten	1 clove garlic, minced
⅓ cup milk	½ teaspoon crushed red pepper flakes
1 cup dried bread crumbs	8 ounces crabmeat
6 speckled trout filets or other white flaky fish	1 teaspoon lemon juice
Salt and pepper	2 dashes Tabasco
3 tablespoons olive oil	2 green onions, chopped
2 tablespoons butter	1 cup Tabasco Cream Sauce (page 10)

Set out three shallow bowls, one for the flour mixed with the Creole spices, one for the eggs mixed with the milk, and the third for the bread crumbs. Season the filets with salt and pepper and dip first in the seasoned flour, then in the egg wash, and then in the bread crumbs.

Heat the oil in a large skillet over medium-high heat. Cook the filets, two at a time, making sure they're cooked through and golden brown on both sides. Remove from the pan, drain on paper towels, and keep warm. Add more oil between batches, if needed.

Drain the pan of excess oil, lower the heat to medium, and add the butter and mushrooms. Cook for a couple of minutes then add the shallots, garlic, and pepper flakes. Stir frequently to make sure the shallot and garlic soften but don't brown. Add the crabmeat, lemon juice, and a little salt and just heat the crabmeat through. Add the Tabasco, fold in the green onions, and remove from the heat.

To serve, place a fish filet on each plate and top with a heaping spoonful of crabmeat and mushrooms. Serve the Tabasco Cream Sauce on the side.

Puppy drum is what we call our small speckled trout, but you can use any white flaky fish. This can be kind of an elegant presentation, topping the filets with crabmeat and mushrooms. I just love wild mushrooms, but use whatever you can find (or afford); even button mushrooms will take on plenty of flavor.

Grilled Redfish with Herb Garlic Butter

✦ Serves 4

❝ These grilled fish filets are so easy to make on the grill, especially if you leave the scales on the skin so it doesn't stick. They're even better with this garlicky herb butter. ❞

2 redfish filets, skin and scales on	Juice of 1 lemon
Salt and pepper	Herb Garlic Butter (page 14)

Heat a grill to medium high. Season the filets with salt and pepper on the flesh side. Place the filets skin-side down on the grill, cover the grill, and cook for 5–7 minutes, until the flesh begins to lift from the skin.

Slice the herb garlic butter and place over the fish filets in a very generous manner. Leave the fish on the grill for about a minute or two, until the butter begins to soften. Using two spatulas, transfer the filets to a serving platter. Carefully spoon the melted butter over the filets and serve.

There's as much speculation about the name of this dish as about the fish it's made with. On New Orleans menus you'll see Trout Amandine or Almondine (the French take, meaning with almonds). But my time cooking in Germany makes me think the name comes from 'les Allemands.' Ours is not freshwater trout, but the much larger saltwater speckled trout, aka spotted weakfish. Whatever you call it, the key is to properly brown the skinless filets slowly and aromatically in butter. Trout meuniere is the same recipe without the almonds.

Trout Almondine

✦ Serves 6

6 6-ounce skinless speckled trout filets	8 tablespoons butter
Salt and pepper	½ cup sliced almonds
1 cup flour	Juice of 1 lemon
1 teaspoon from My Creole Spice Jar (page xi)	2 tablespoons minced fresh parsley

Season the fish filets well with salt and pepper. Mix the flour with the Creole Spices in a shallow bowl and dredge the filets in the seasoned flour.

Melt 4 tablespoons of the butter in a large skillet over medium-high heat. Add the filets and cook on each side until golden brown, about 3 minutes per side. Transfer the fish to a serving platter.

Add the remaining 4 tablespoons butter to the same skillet, swirling it over medium-high heat so the butter melts evenly and takes on a brownish hue, 5-7 minutes. Reduce the heat to medium low, add the almonds, and cook, stirring gently, until the nuts are toasty brown, about 3 minutes. Add the lemon juice, parsley, and a dash of salt. Spoon the browned butter and almonds over the fish and serve right from the pan.

BEEF — Per LB

Item	Price
~~Blade Eye~~	$9
~~Blade Steak~~	$12
~~Bones, Marrow~~	$10
Bones, Pet/Stock	$3
Bottom Round	$8
Brisket	$10
Chuck	$9
Chuck Eye	$14
~~Deckle~~	$9
Fat/Suet	$5
Flank	$11
Flatiron	$15
Ground/Stew	$8
~~Hanger~~	$21
Heart	$8
Kidney	$4
Liver	$6
Neck	$8
~~Neck Tender~~	$10
~~Oxtail~~	$8
Porterhouse	$23
Ribeye	$21
Round	$8
~~Rump Cap~~	$14
~~Shank~~	$8
Short Ribs	$9
~~Shoulder Tender~~	$15
~~Sirloin~~	$15
Skirt	$12
~~Spinalis~~	$27
Spleen	$4
Strip	$21
~~Sweetbreads~~	$12
Tallow	$6
Tenderloin	$27
Tendon	$3
Tongue	$12
Top Blade	$15
Top Round	$8
~~Tri-Tip~~	$14

GONSOULIN — NEW IBERIA, LA
LAND & CATTLE

PORK — Per LB

Item	Price
Belly	$10
Bone	$2
Fatback	$8
Ground/Stew	$8
~~Ham Steak~~	$7
Heart	$10
Jowls	$5
Kidney	$6
Lard	$7
Liver	$7
Loin Chops	$12
Loin Roast	$12
Picnic	$10
~~Porterhouse~~	$14
Ribs	$10
~~Round~~	$8
Shank	$5
Shoulder	$10
Sirloin	$10
Skin	$3
Skirt	$10
Spleen	$5
~~Tenderloin~~	$15
Tongue	$7
Trotters	$4

CHAPPAPEELA FARMS — LA

Dog

Dog Food ... $4/lb

Dog Bones ... $3/lb

Dog Treats ... $5 ea.

BUTCHER SHOP

❝ My smokehouse pays homage to the one my Grandaddy Walters had at 'The Home Place' on a farm near Slidell; our practices are the same as those that sustained our people for centuries. We save the blood from hogs to make boudin noir. We cure, age, and lightly smoke our country hams. We cure pork bellies in sea salt and Louisiana brown sugar, then double-smoke them over pecan wood. ❞

EN /DUCK

. . $5
. . $9
. . $5
. X . $8
. X . $8
. . $8
. . $8
. X . $6

X $6
X $12
X $7
$8
$9
$8
$—
$8
$—

ms Chappapeela Farms
LR Husser, LA

LAMB

Belly
Bones
Ground/Stew
Head
Heart
Kidneys
Leaf Fat
Leg
Liver/Spleen
Neck
Rack
Ribs
Saddle
Shank
Shoulder
Tongue
Bayou Fa

UTERIE

Muscles $25/lb
Pancetta
Figeeo
Lardo
Sirloin

IT. . $9/lb

FARMS
ANDY HOOK, MS

EAKS

per lb

. . $19
. . $29
. . $29

Weekend

FRES
CR
Saturday
$5/quart

❝ Every little roadside meat market in Cajun country has these sausage-stuffed pork chops. The key to making them at home is to find thick, luscious chops that will take deep cuts to make roomy pockets to stuff. ❞

Cajun Stuffed Pork Chops

✦ Serves 4

2 tablespoons bacon fat or oil
1 onion, chopped
1 stalk celery, chopped
3 cloves garlic, minced
½ pound pork sausage, removed from casing
¼ cup Go-Chicken Stock (page 27) or water
1 egg, beaten

½ cup Italian dried bread crumbs
1 teaspoon crushed red pepper flakes
4 center-cut pork chops, about 2 inches thick
Salt and pepper
2 tablespoons canola oil

Preheat the oven to 350°. Heat the bacon fat in a large skillet over medium-high heat and add the onions. Cook, stirring, for 5 minutes or until the onions begin to brown. Add the celery and garlic and continue to cook for another 3–5 minutes. Transfer the onion mixture to a large bowl and mix in the sausage, stock, egg, bread crumbs, and pepper flakes.

Create a large pocket in each of the pork chops with a small knife, cutting the meat in half just to the bone. Fill each of the pork chops with the sausage stuffing and season the outsides with plenty of salt and pepper.

Sear the chops in the oil in a large ovenproof skillet over medium-high heat until golden brown on both sides. Place the skillet in the oven and bake for 15–20 minutes, until the chops are cooked through.

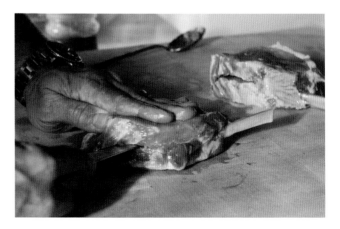

I love the surprise when you cut into a thick, meaty pork chop and discover the stuffing. It could be green onion sausage, andouille, bacon, even crawfish.

Everything about making this dish is such a sensory experience: the act of cutting the peppers and saving the tops to chop for a gumbo or stew, the tactile feeling of stuffing each pepper with my hands, the way the stuffed multi-colored peppers look in the pan, and the gorgeous aroma after they've baked. Such a delicious and easy way to manufacture dinner.

Creole Stuffed Bell Peppers

✦ Serves 6-8

1 pound pork sausage, removed from casings

1 onion, chopped

4 cloves garlic, minced

1 teaspoon crushed red pepper flakes

1 teaspoon dried thyme
Salt and pepper

¾ cup uncooked white rice

3½ cups Cherry Tomato Five-Minute Sauce (page 84) or other good tomato sauce

8 bell peppers, different colors if possible, tops cut off and seeded

2 tablespoons olive oil

Preheat the oven to 325°. Mix the sausage meat with the onions, garlic, pepper flakes, thyme, salt, and pepper a large bowl. Stir in the rice and 1½ cups of the tomato sauce. Suff each bell pepper with the mixture, mounding it over the tops.

Pour the remaining 2 cups tomato sauce into a small baking dish. Fit the peppers upright in the baking dish snugly, shoulder to shoulder. Sprinkle on salt and pepper, and drizzle with the olive oil. Cover with foil and bake for about 45 minutes. Uncover and let the stuffing brown for another few minutes. Serve in shallow bowls with plenty of the tasty juices.

❝ Celeste figs were the favorite of my Grandaddy Walters— the only fig he knew in fact—and he proudly put up jars and jars of them every season. Just figs, no spices. Use any kind of preserved figs here. They'd be just as luxurious with a pork loin. ❞

Seared Venison with Fig Preserves

✦ Serves 4-6

2 pounds venison loin	1 shallot, minced
Salt	1 clove garlic, minced
Sugar	1 teaspoon minced peeled fresh ginger
Pepper	¾ cup rice wine vinegar
2 teaspoons canola oil	1 cup fig preserves

Trim the silverskin from the venison and cut into 6-inch lengths. Make a brine in a bowl, whisking to dissolve enough salt in warm water so it tastes like sea water, then adding just enough sugar to sweeten it. Submerge the venison in the brine and refrigerate for 30 minutes.

Remove the venison from the brine and pat dry with paper towels. Season with a touch of salt and pepper. Heat the oil in a cast iron skillet over high heat, add the venison pieces, and cook so that they brown well on the outside and are rare in the middle. Remove the venison from the pan and keep warm.

Make the sauce in the same skillet: Add the shallots, garlic, and ginger and reduce the heat to medium. Stir for a moment, then add the vinegar and fig preserves. Stir until the preserves dissolve. Season with salt and pepper.

To serve, slice the venison into medallions and spoon the fig sauce over the top.

> ❝ It so pleases me when one of my boys finds a thing he likes to cook. My youngest son, Andrew, loves to make these easy cutlets. Sometimes we use slices from a pork loin, but often we'll use turkey cutlets. ❞

Andrew's Pan-Fried Pork Cutlets

✦ Serves 4-6

- 1 2-pound pork loin, cut into 1-inch cutlets
  Salt and pepper
- 1 cup flour
- 2 eggs, beaten
- 1 cup milk
- 2 cups dried bread crumbs
  Canola oil
- 1 lemon, halved

Lay a piece of plastic wrap over a cutting board, place the cutlets on the board, and cover with another layer of plastic wrap. Using a meat mallet or a heavy pan, pound the cutlets until they're ¼ to ½ inch thick. Season with salt and pepper.

Set out three shallow bowls. Put the flour in one, mix the eggs and milk together in the second, and put the bread crumbs into the third. When ready to cook, dip each cutlet into the flour, then the egg/milk mixture, and then into the bread crumbs.

Heat ¼ inch oil in a large heavy skillet over medium-high heat. Add the breaded cutlets in batches and cook until golden brown on each side. Remove from the pan, and add salt and a squeeze of lemon juice.

> **❝** Sometimes nothing is easier than a big roast, and I often make one on Sunday to take us through the week. A simple gravy made from the pan drippings and the vegetables that cook with the roast adds rich flavor with hardly any effort. **❞**

Perfect Roast Pork Shoulder with Country Gravy

✦ Serves 8

1 5-pound boneless pork shoulder	Big pinch crushed red pepper flakes
Salt and pepper	2 tablespoons flour
3 garlic cloves, thinly sliced	1 shallot, minced
2 onions, chopped	3 cups Go-To Chicken Stock (page 27) or water
1 carrot, peeled and chopped	
1 stalk celery, chopped	1 sprig thyme

Preheat the oven to 325°. Season the shoulder liberally with salt and pepper. Stand the roast on a board, fat side up. With a paring knife, make many small incisions in the roast and insert a slice of garlic into each.

Scatter the onions, carrots, celery, and pepper flakes in a roasting pan. Set the shoulder on top and add 2 cups water. Roast for about 2½ hours, until the pork registers 145° on a meat thermometer. Let the meat rest for 15 minutes; reserve the pan with the drippings and vegetables.

For the country gravy, heat 2 tablespoons of the fat from the pan in a small saucepan over medium-high heat. Whisk in the flour and keep whisking for 3 minutes. Add the shallots and stir for a couple of minutes, then whisk in the stock so no lumps form. Stir in the vegetables from the roasting pan, bring to a boil, reduce the heat to medium low, and add the thyme, salt, and pepper. Let the sauce simmer for a few minutes, then serve with the pork shoulder.

ff Fried chicken always makes me think of the great ladies I've known. In New Orleans, it's Miss Willie Mae Seaton, who ran Willie Mae's Scotch House in the Treme, and the awesome Miss Leah Chase at Dooky Chase's Restaurant, right around the corner. Miss Leah's fried chicken is much like my Grandmother Grace's—it's the fried chicken I grew up on. She used a classic buttermilk batter to give each piece its super crunchy texture. **JJ**

Grandmother Grace's Fried Chicken

✦ Serves 6

1 chicken, cut into 8 pieces	1 teaspoon garlic powder
Salt and pepper	½ teaspoon cayenne pepper
1 quart buttermilk	Canola oil
3 cups flour	
1 teaspoon celery salt	

Season the chicken pieces generously with salt and pepper. In a large bowl, soak the chicken in the buttermilk for at least 15 minutes. The idea is that the lactic acids tenderize the chicken. Sometimes my grandmother would even put the soaking chicken in the fridge overnight.

Mix together the flour, celery salt, garlic powder, cayenne, salt, and pepper in a large bowl. Dredge each chicken piece in the seasoned flour to coat well. The batter should just barely adhere to the chicken, so make sure you give each piece a little shake to let extra batter drop off before frying.

Heat about 1 inch of canola oil in a heavy skillet until it reaches 350˚. Place a few pieces of the chicken in the oil at a time and fry for 6–8 minutes. Using a slotted spoon, turn each piece over, then cover the pan to cook for an additional 6 minutes. (After the chicken was in the hot oil, my grandmother would put the lid on her pot and a kind of pressure cooker thing began to happen inside—the meat inside gets to cook, leaving the outside crispy.) Drain on paper towels and salt well.

BUTCHER SHOP

❝ Sometimes my wife, Jenifer, will make corn bread (page 129) especially to stuff a chicken and other times she'll just use whatever corn bread we have left over. Shrimp works well in this stuffing, too. ❞

Jenny's Crawfish-Stuffed Chicken

✦ Serves 8

2 tablespoons bacon fat or oil

¼ pound andouille or other smoked sausage, chopped

¼ pound hot pork sausage, removed from casing

1 onion, chopped

1 stalk celery, chopped

2 cloves garlic, minced

2 cups peeled and chopped crawfish tails

6 cups crumbled corn bread

2 cups Go-To Chicken Stock (page 27)

½ cup heavy cream

2 eggs, lightly beaten

2 tablespoons chopped fresh parsley

2 green onions, chopped

1 jalapeño pepper, minced

Salt and pepper

2 whole chickens (about 4 pounds each)

2 tablespoons olive oil

2 teaspoons herbes de Provence

To prepare the stuffing, heat the bacon fat and cook the andouille and pork sausage in a large skillet over medium-high heat, breaking up the pork with the back of a spoon. When the meat has browned, add the onions, celery, and garlic and cook, stirring occasionally, until the onions are translucent, about 5 minutes.

Add the crawfish and cook for 2 minutes more. Transfer the mixture to a large mixing bowl and stir in the corn bread, stock, cream, eggs, parsley, green onions, jalapeño, salt, and pepper until well combined.

Preheat the oven to 400°. Rub the chickens with the olive oil and season inside and out with salt and pepper. Stuff each chicken with the crawfish dressing and dust the outsides with the herbes de Provence.

Place the chickens on a rack in a large roasting pan; add a half inch of water to the pan. Roast until the chickens are golden brown and the juices run clear when the birds are pricked, about 50 minutes.

❝ I'm always amazed how many regional products still endure in this homogenized country of ours. One of the best is our pepper jelly. I'll use it to make the Pepper Jelly Glaze, right, or a vinaigrette (mixing ½ cup jelly with ½ cup red wine vinegar, a teaspoon of sambal chili paste, and 1½ cups oil), or just serve it on the side with a juicy roast. Order pepper jelly from Tabasco.com in mild or spicy flavors. For this roast, it's important to find 6-pound ducks. Smaller ones can be tough and dry. ❞

Crispy Roast Ducklings with Pepper Jelly Glaze

✦ Serves 6

2 bay leaves
1 head garlic, halved
2 6-pound ducks
1 tablespoon dried thyme
Salt and pepper
2 onions, chopped

2 stalks celery, chopped
1 carrot, peeled and chopped
Pepper Jelly Glaze

Preheat the oven to 325°. Place a bay leaf and a half of the head of garlic in the cavity of each duck and tie their legs together with butchers' string. Season generously on all sides with the thyme, salt, and pepper.

Spread the onions, celery, and carrots in the bottom of a roasting pan and pour in water to cover. Set the ducks on the vegetables, breast side up. Roast for about 2 hours, until the ducks' skin is mahogany. Let the ducks rest for 30 minutes before carving. Save the pan drippings for the glaze.

PEPPER JELLY GLAZE

✦ Makes about 1½ cups

In a small saucepan, mix 1 cup pepper jelly, ½ cup vinegar, 1 minced shallot, and 1 minced clove garlic with ½ cup drippings from the roasting pan and heat for 10 minutes.

Serve the pepper jelly glaze over the carved ducks.

SWEETNESS

Our old sweet shops are iconic statements of New Orleans life. Angelo Brocato began his Sicilian ice cream shop in the French Quarter in 1905, then moved to the site of the present Croissant d'Or Patisserie (page 191), where the Angelo Brocato sidewalk tile 'Ladies entrance' exists today. Brocato's, now in Mid-City, is still the place for Sicilian ices, gelato, and cannoli. It's where we buy our favorite brightly colored St. Joseph's Day cookies (page 187): biscotti with sesame seeds and cucidati, fig cookies with sprinkles.

❝ To me, apple pie is nowhere near as iconic as blueberry. Just look at this pie! I love blueberry pie hot, just out of the oven, but around our house, the boys have been known to eat it for breakfast. You can bake this as one big pie, or divide the dough and filling among 6 individual 3- or 4-inch tart pans. ❞

Simple as Blueberry Pie

✦ Makes one 9-inch pie

4 tablespoons butter, softened	1 egg
3 tablespoons all-purpose flour, plus more for rolling	3 cups blueberries
1 disk Go-To Pie Dough (page 179)	1 teaspoon freshly grated lemon zest
½ cup granulated sugar	Confectioners' sugar, for serving
¼ teaspoon salt	

Preheat the oven to 375°. Butter a 9-inch pie pan with 1 tablespoon of the softened butter. Dust the pan with 1 tablespoon of the flour.

Roll out the dough on a floured surface to a thickness of ¼ inch. Wrap the dough around the rolling pin, then gently fit the dough into the pan. Trim off excess dough and crimp the edges.

Beat together the remaining 3 tablespoons butter, the granulated sugar, salt, and egg in a mixing bowl until smooth and creamy. Fold in the blueberries, the remaining 2 tablespoons flour, and lemon zest. Fill the pie shell. Transfer the pie to a baking sheet and bake until the crust is golden brown, about 20 minutes. Dust with a touch of confectioners' sugar.

Gelato

VANILLA BEAN	RUM RAISIN
CHOCOLATE	MOCHA
STRAWBERRY	ZUPPA INGLESE
PISTACHIO ALMOND	AMARETTO
PISTACHIO NUT	PRALINE
STRACCIATELLA	COCONUT
BACI (ITALIAN KISS)	STRAWBERRY CHEESECAKE
TIRA MI SU	MINT CHIP

Granita · Italian Ices

STRAWBERRY	LEMON	RASPBERRY

CUPS and CONES   Small   Large

Hand Packed Gelato

Pint   Quert

ANGELO BROCATO
SINCE 1905
Italian Specialty Gelato

PORTIONS		PRE-PACKED QUARTS TO GO	
Spumoni		Spumoni c&r	
Cassata		Cassata c&r	
Torroncino		Torroncino	
Bisquit		Pistachio ALMOND	
Tortoni		Vanilla	
Cappuccino		Chocolate	
Ice Cream Pie		Lemon Ice	
Sciallotti		Strawberry Ice	
Coppa Gelato		Raspberry Ice	

PRE-PACKED PINTS

Chocolate Ice	Mango Ice	Orange Ice

Go-To Pie Dough

✦ Makes 2 disks (for one 9-inch pie with a top and bottom crust or two single-crust pies)

❝ No pie dough has stood the test of time in our kitchens as well as this one. I am proud to pass it along, with just one caveat: do not overwork the dough! I always make enough for two crusts, freezing one disk if I don't need it right away. When I want to use the frozen dough, I just thaw it in the refrigerator overnight. ❞

2 cups all-purpose flour, plus more for dusting

2 teaspoons granulated sugar

½ teaspoon salt

14 tablespoons cold butter, diced, plus more for buttering the pan

About ½ cup ice water

Whisk together the flour, sugar, and salt in a large bowl. Cut the butter into the flour with 2 knives until it resembles cornmeal. Sprinkle in ice water as needed (up to 8 tablespoons) to help the dough come together.

Gather into two balls, press into round, flat disks, and wrap each one well in plastic wrap. Refrigerate 30 minutes or freeze for later use.

When our Louisiana peaches are in season, there's no better dessert than a peach pie.
My dear friend Suzanne Krieger makes fabulous peach pies. She freezes them unbaked and gives them as presents.
My boys know her as 'The Peach Lady!'

Suzanne's Peach Pie

✦ Makes one 9-inch pie

5 tablespoons butter, softened

5 tablespoons all-purpose flour, plus more for rolling

2 disks Go-To Pie Dough (page 179)

4 large or 7 small ripe peaches, peeled and sliced

Juice of ½ lemon

½ cup granulated sugar

½ teaspoon cinnamon

Preheat the oven to 350°. Butter a 9-inch pie pan with 1 tablespoon of the softened butter. Dust the pan with 1 tablespoon of the flour.

Roll out each disk of dough on a floured surface to a thickness of ¼ inch. Cut one sheet of rolled dough into strips ¾ inch wide for the lattice top, transfer the strips to a baking sheet, and refrigerate until ready to assemble the pie. Wrap the dough for the bottom crust around the rolling pin, then gently fit it into the pan and trim off excess.

Toss the peaches with the lemon juice in a mixing bowl. Stir together the remaining 4 tablespoons flour, the sugar, and cinnamon in a small bowl. Add to peaches and toss well. Spoon the peach mixture into prepared pie shell. Thinly slice the remaining 4 tablespoons butter on top of the peaches. Remove the dough strips from the refrigerator and weave them into a lattice top. Don't worry if it's not perfect!

Set the pie on a baking sheet to catch drips and bake for at least 1 hour, until the crust is light brown and the filling has thickened.

SWEETNESS

> My boys love to scour the woods for wild berries—blackberries, raspberries, dewberries—any berry will work for this pie, as will, of course, store-bought berries. We use Creole cream cheese as our cream base, but crème fraîche, sour cream, or Greek yogurt are perfect substitutes. Taste the filling and add a bit more sugar if you use sour cream or yogurt. Again, don't work the pie dough too much. Roll it out and be really, really gentle. "

Wild Berry Cream Pie

✦ Makes one 9-inch pie

1 disk Go-To Pie Dough (page 179)	1 teaspoon salt
1 cup Creole cream cheese	5 cups berries
1 cup granulated sugar	¼ cup graham cracker crumbs
3 tablespoons all-purpose flour, plus more for dusting and rolling	3 tablespoons brown sugar
Grated zest of 1 orange	2 tablespoons butter, plus more for the pan, softened

Preheat the oven to 375°. Liberally butter a 9-inch pie pan, then dust with flour. Roll out the dough on a floured surface to a thickness of ¼ inch. Wrap the dough around the rolling pin, then gently fit the dough into the pan. Trim off excess dough and crimp the edges.

Mix together the cream cheese, granulated sugar, flour, orange zest, and salt in a large bowl until well combined. Fold the berries into the cheese mixture, crushing some of them. Spoon the filling into the pie shell and bake for 30 minutes.

Meanwhile, combine the graham cracker crumbs with the brown sugar and butter in a small mixing bowl. Mix well and set aside.

When the pie has baked for 30 minutes, remove it from the oven, crumble the graham cracker topping over the surface, and return to the oven for 15 minutes more. Let the pie cool before serving.

Blackberry Crumble

✦ Serves 8

❝ This dessert is the easiest thing to put together, yet it's real cooking. I love to make it in a gratin dish or in little ramekins and serve it right from the oven, while it's still bubbling. Hard to imagine a better way to end a meal than a hot berry crumble and a scoop (or two) of vanilla ice cream. This recipe is so forgiving, you can make the crumble with almost any fruit. ❞

FRUIT

- 1 pound blackberries
- 3 tablespoons brown sugar
- 2 tablespoons all-purpose flour
- 2 tablespoons butter, melted
- 1 egg, lightly beaten
- 1½ tablespoons bourbon
  Grated zest of 2 lemons
  Pinch cinnamon

CRUMBLE

- ⅔ cup all-purpose flour
- ⅓ cup packed brown sugar
- ¼ cup granulated sugar
- ½ teaspoon cinnamon
  Pinch salt
- 6 tablespoons butter, cut into ½-inch pieces

Preheat the oven to 400°. To prepare the fruit, toss the blackberries in a mixing bowl with the brown sugar, flour, melted butter, egg, bourbon, zest, and cinnamon and coat well. Spoon the mixture into one baking dish or individual ramekins.

To make the crumble, combine the flour, sugars, cinnamon, and salt in a mixing bowl. Cut the butter into the mixture with 2 knives until the topping is crumbly. Sprinkle over the fruit. Bake until the fruit is bubbly and the topping turns a lovely golden brown, about 25 minutes.

This fruit dessert only works when the best local fruit is in season. With fruit that fresh, almost any combination is great, so substitute whatever you like. Just toss the cut fruit with the Champagne and mint. Even better, if there's leftover fruit, puree and freeze it to make a delicious sorbet.

Peaches & Blueberries with Champagne

Serves 8-10

1 cup Champagne
¼ cup sugar
2 tablespoons minced fresh mint leaves

2 cups blueberries (or other berries)
2 cups sliced peeled peaches

Whisk together the Champagne, sugar, and mint in a small bowl. Select a beautiful serving bowl and spoon in the blueberries and peaches. Pour the Champagne mixture over the fruit and toss gently to mix.

❑ This dessert celebrates Louisiana's famed Celeste and Southeastern Brown Turkey figs in a brown butter custard that's so good it borders on sinful. I've been told that you can find figs just as succulent in other parts of the country. ❑❑

Rustic Fig Tart

✦ Makes one 9-inch tart

9 tablespoons butter

1 disk Go-To Pie Dough (page 179)

3 eggs, beaten

1 cup granulated sugar

½ cup all-purpose flour, plus more for dusting and rolling

1 teaspoon grated orange zest

1 teaspoon vanilla extract

Pinch salt

2 pints ripe figs, quartered or halved

Preheat the oven to 350°. Butter a deep tart mold or cake pan with 1 tablespoon of the butter and dust with a bit of flour.

Roll out the dough on a floured surface to a thickness of ¼ inch. Wrap the dough around the rolling pin, then gently fit the dough into the pan. Trim off excess dough.

Melt the remaining 8 tablespoons butter in a small saucepan over medium-high heat until it has a nutty aroma and deep golden brown color. Remove the brown butter from the heat.

Cream the eggs and sugar together in a mixing bowl with an electric hand mixer until light and fluffy, about 5 minutes. Fold in the flour, zest, vanilla, and salt by hand. Slowly stir in all of the brown butter. Pour the mixture into the pan. Layer in all the figs, overlapping them in a circular pattern.

Bake until the crust is golden brown and the custard has nearly set in the center of the tart, 35–40 minutes. Let cool on a wire rack for 15–20 minutes before serving.

" If there was an American version of *appellation contrôlée*, Ponchatoula strawberries would surely qualify. Unlike most of our supersize, cottony American berries, strawberries from Ponchatoula taste wonderful, especially on flaky biscuits just like my Grandmother Walters used to make. **"**

Strawberry Shortcakes with Vanilla Sauce

✦ Serves 8

VANILLA SAUCE

- 1 cup Creole cream cheese
- ⅓ cup heavy cream
- 3 tablespoons granulated sugar
  Seeds from ½ vanilla bean (save the pod for the strawberries)

BISCUITS

- 2 cups all-purpose flour, plus more for rolling
- ¼ cup granulated sugar
- 2 tablespoons baking powder
  Pinch salt
  Grated zest of 1 lemon
- 6 tablespoons cold butter, diced
  About ¾ cup whole milk

BERRIES

- 2 pints strawberries, hulled and diced
- ¼ cup granulated sugar
- 2 tablespoons Grand Marnier
- 2 teaspoons lemon juice
- ½ vanilla bean pod
- 1 tablespoon fresh minced mint leaves

  Confectioners' sugar, for serving

To make the sauce, whisk together the cream cheese, heavy cream, granulated sugar, and vanilla bean seeds in a medium mixing bowl until well combined. Cover and refrigerate.

To make the biscuits, preheat the oven to 400°. Combine the flour, sugar, baking powder, salt, and lemon zest in a mixing bowl. Cut the butter into the flour with a fork until the texture resembles cornmeal. Gradually stir in just enough milk for the dough to form a ball. Don't overwork the dough or the biscuits will be tough.

Roll out the dough on a lightly floured surface to a thickness of about ¾ inch and cut out 8 disks with a cookie cutter or glass. Place the biscuits on a baking sheet at least an inch apart. Bake until golden brown, 12–15 minutes. Set aside to let cool.

To make the berries, toss the strawberries, granulated sugar, Grand Marnier, lemon juice, vanilla bean pod, and mint together in a medium bowl. Cover and refrigerate for at least 30 minutes or up to 6 hours.

To assemble a shortcake, halve a biscuit crosswise and set the bottom half on a dessert plate, cut side up. Spoon some berries over the biscuit, then top with a spoonful or two of vanilla sauce. Lean the top jauntily on the berries and dust with confectioners' sugar.

❝ I forever associate angel food cake with enforced quiet: my mother would always tell us kids that if we made noise while it was baking, the cake would not rise. And I'll admit to using that same line with my own boys. The great thing about this cake is that it seems to last for days. As it becomes a touch stale, it's perfect for absorbing the juices from the jasmine tea–soaked berries. ❞

Angel Food Cake with Tea-Soaked Berries

✦ Serves 8-10

CAKE

- 1 cup cake flour
- 1½ cups granulated sugar
- 1¼ cups egg whites, from about 10 large eggs, at room temperature
- 1 teaspoon cream of tartar
- 1 teaspoon vanilla extract
- ¼ teaspoon salt
- ½ cup finely chopped white chocolate

BERRIES

- ¾ cup granulated sugar
- Grated zest of 1 lemon
- 1 teaspoon jasmine tea leaves
- ½ cup blueberries
- ½ cup blackberries
- ½ cup strawberries
- ½ cup raspberries

Confectioners' sugar for dusting

Preheat the oven to 350°. Arrange the oven racks so that the cake will fit on the lowest rack.

To make the cake, sift together the cake flour and ½ cup of the sugar in a mixing bowl and set aside. In the bowl of a stand mixer fitted with the whisk attachment, whip the egg whites until foamy. Add the cream of tartar, vanilla, and salt. With the mixer on medium-high speed, add the remaining 1 cup sugar in a steady stream. Continue whipping the egg whites until stiff peaks form.

Remove the bowl from the mixer and carefully fold in the sifted flour and sugar, a little bit at a time, just until fully incorporated. Stir in the white chocolate.

Gently pour the batter into an ungreased 10-inch Bundt pan. Knock the pan on the counter a few times to release air bubbles. Bake the cake until lightly golden and dry, about 40 minutes. Remove the pan from the oven and invert it. Allow the cake to cool completely before releasing it from the pan.

For the berries, combine ½ cup water, the sugar, lemon zest, and tea leaves in a medium saucepan and boil over medium-high heat until the sugar dissolves. Strain out the tea leaves and return the syrup to the pan. Add the blueberries and blackberries and poach over low heat for 2 minutes. Remove from the heat and add the strawberries. Let cool, then add the raspberries. Refrigerate until ready to serve.

Just before serving, dust the cake with confectioners' sugar and fill the center with the tea-soaked berries.

There are so many savory ways to use our Louisiana rice, sometimes we forget the luscious and oh so comforting rice pudding. I love to make it with fresh fruit, but when none is in season, I use a great variety of dried fruit (see Variation), which is so good you almost forget about the fresh.

Stone Fruit Rice Pudding

✦ Serves 6

4	cups milk	1	cup granulated sugar
	Grated zest of 1 orange	4	egg yolks
1	teaspoon vanilla extract	½	cup cherries, pitted and halved
1	teaspoon cinnamon		
½	teaspoon salt	½	cup chopped peaches
1	cup uncooked rice	½	cup chopped plums
6	tablespoons butter	½	cup chopped apricots

Combine the milk, orange zest, vanilla, cinnamon, and salt in a medium saucepan and bring to a boil over medium heat. Add the rice and cook for about 30 minutes.

Preheat the oven to 325°. Butter a large, deep baking dish with 2 tablespoons of the butter.

In a large mixing bowl, cream the remaining 4 tablespoons butter and the granulated sugar until light and fluffy. Add the egg yolks one at a time, incorporating well after each addition. Carefully fold the rice mixture into the egg mixture, then add the fruit.

Pour the mixture into the prepared baking dish. Set the baking dish into a larger pan filled with hot water to come halfway up the sides. Bake the pudding in this water bath until just set, about 30 minutes. Carefully remove from the oven. Rice pudding should be served hot with a crispy top.

VARIATION

Dried Fruit Rice Pudding

Substitute the following dried fruit for the fresh in the above recipe.

½	cup dried tart cherries, chopped	½	cup dried dates, pitted and chopped
½	cup dried apricots, chopped	½	cup prunes, pitted and chopped

In all the cultural brouhaha surrounding our city, we sometimes forget that New Orleans is a wildly busy port, one of the biggest in the country. So it's not so surprising that the bananas and rum that are shipped in from the south are combined in one of our most beloved desserts, one made even more showy for the flaming finale at the table. I find that last bit optional! Vanilla ice cream, however, is not.

Bananas Foster

✦ Serves 6

8 tablespoons butter
½ cup lightly packed brown sugar
1 teaspoon cinnamon
   Pinch ground nutmeg
3 tablespoons orange juice

6 bananas, peeled, halved lengthwise and then crosswise
½ cup dark rum

Heat the butter and brown sugar in a large skillet over high heat, stirring until they have melted into a caramel. Cook 3 minutes more, stirring constantly. Stir in the cinnamon, nutmeg, and orange juice, then add the bananas. Cook for 3 minutes, stirring gently to coat the bananas and spooning the sauce over them.

Remove the pan from the heat and, holding the skillet away from you, carefully add the rum. Return the skillet to heat and cook for another 3 minutes. Be aware that the alcohol may ignite if you're cooking over an open flame. If you're into the pyrotechnics, use a match to burn off the alcohol. Serve immediately on individual plates, spooning the sauce over the bananas.

> Mamma's Bread Pudding is a quintessential New Orleans dessert. It looks as good as it tastes and tastes as good as it smells. I make it every chance I get.

> Do you have to make this bread pudding with French bread? Well, that's the bread we get in New Orleans—those light, fluffy loaves, like Leidenheimer's, are the ones we make po'boys from, and it's what my mamma uses. They make an unbelievable bread pudding. Of course any bread will make a pudding characteristic of that bread. I like to keep the bread in the egg mixture till a bit soupy—that's the perfect consistency. And the buttery rum sauce? 'Nuff said.

Mamma's Bread Pudding with Hot Buttered Rum Sauce

✦ Serves 8–10

BREAD PUDDING

- 4 cups milk
- 2 cups heavy cream
- 11 eggs
- 1½ cups granulated sugar
- 1½ teaspoons cinnamon
- 1 teaspoon vanilla extract
  Grated zest of 1 orange
- 4 cups cubed stale bread
- 2 tablespoons butter

RUM SAUCE

- 8 tablespoons butter
- ½ cup light corn syrup
- 1 cup granulated sugar
- 1 cup dark rum
- ¾ cup heavy cream
- 1 teaspoon vanilla extract
  Salt

To make the pudding, whisk together the milk, cream, eggs, sugar, cinnamon, vanilla, and zest in a large mixing bowl. Stir in the bread cubes and soak for at least 30 minutes (longer is fine).

Preheat the oven to 350°. Butter a large baking dish with the butter. Pour the bread mixture into the prepared dish and bake until crispy and golden, about 45 minutes.

Meanwhile, to make the sauce, melt the butter in a medium saucepan over medium heat until it turns a light brown color, with a rich nutty aroma, about 5 minutes. Add the corn syrup, sugar, rum, cream, vanilla, and salt. Reduce the sauce until it thickens enough to coat the back of a spoon, about 15 minutes. Remove from the heat.

Pour the buttered rum sauce over the pudding and serve it up!

ACKNOWLEDGMENTS

Our team, from left: Erick Loos, Kelly Fields, Dorothy Kalins, Kim Bourgault, moi, Maggie Moore, Brian Landry, Maura McEvoy. Not pictured: Don Morris.

Were it not for the passionate and talented efforts of my dear friend Dorothy Kalins, *Besh Big Easy* would only be a dream. I will never be able to thank Maura McEvoy enough for her keen eye and dreamy photographs that tell the story of my food. I will forever be in awe of Don Morris, whose art direction has transformed my thoughts, recipes, and vision into four incredible books.

I would be remiss if I didn't acknowledge and thank my publisher and friends at Andrews McMeel Publishing, especially the extremely talented Kirsty Melville, who believed in our vision for each of our beautiful cookbooks. At AMP I'm grateful, too, to our editors, Jean Lucas and Maureen Sullivan, and to Tim Lynch and Carol Coe. Thanks to the great editorial eyes of Deri Reed, Kathy Brennan, and

Sue Li. And to David Black for believing in the potential of *Besh Big Easy.* I'm so very indebted to my wonderful team of Maggie Moore, Kim Bourgault, Emery Whalen, Erick Loos, and Brian Landry for their support in organizing, testing, and photographing my 101 favorite New Orleans recipes. I am grateful for the delicious efforts of the *über*talented and soulful pastry goddess Kelly Fields, who has continually helped me create approachable desserts for all of my menus, books, and whims. Most of all, I would like to thank my wonderful wife, Jenifer, who has relentlessly supported the many books, restaurants, and passions of mine.

METRIC CONVERSIONS & EQUIVALENTS

Approximate Metric Equivalents

Volume	Metric
¼ teaspoon	1 milliliter
½ teaspoon	2.5 milliliters
¾ teaspoon	4 milliliters
1 teaspoon	5 milliliters
1¼ teaspoons	6 milliliters
1½ teaspoons	7.5 milliliters
1¾ teaspoons	8.5 milliliters
2 teaspoons	10 milliliters
1 tablespoon (½ fluid ounce)	15 milliliters
2 tablespoons (1 fluid ounce)	30 milliliters
¼ cup	60 milliliters
⅓ cup	80 milliliters
½ cup (4 fluid ounces)	120 milliliters
⅔ cup	160 milliliters
¾ cup	180 milliliters
1 cup (8 fluid ounces)	240 milliliters
1¼ cups	300 milliliters
1½ cups (12 fluid ounces)	360 milliliters
1⅔ cups	400 milliliters
2 cups (1 pint)	460 milliliters
3 cups	700 milliliters
4 cups (1 quart)	0.95 liter
1 quart plus ¼ cup	1 liter
4 quarts (1 gallon)	3.8 liters

Weight	Metric
¼ ounce	7 grams
½ ounce	14 grams
¾ ounce	21 grams
1 ounce	28 grams
1¼ ounces	35 grams
1½ ounces	42.5 grams
1⅔ ounces	45 grams
2 ounces	57 grams
3 ounces	85 grams
4 ounces (¼ pound)	113 grams
5 ounces	142 grams
6 ounces	170 grams
7 ounces	198 grams
8 ounces (½ pound)	227 grams
16 ounces (1 pound)	454 grams
35.25 ounces (2.2 pounds)	1 kilogram

Length	Metric
⅛ inch	3 millimeters
¼ inch	6 millimeters
½ inch	1¼ centimeters
1 inch	2½ centimeters
2 inches	5 centimeters
2½ inches	6 centimeters
4 inches	10 centimeters
5 inches	13 centimeters
6 inches	15¼ centimeters
12 inches (1 foot)	30 centimeters

Metric Conversion Formulas

To Convert	Multiply
Ounces to grams	Ounces by 28.35
Pounds to kilograms	Pounds by .454
Teaspoons to milliliters	Teaspoons by 4.93
Tablespoons to milliliters	Tablespoons by 14.79
Fluid ounces to milliliters	Fluid ounces by 29.57
Cups to milliliters	Cups by 236.59
Cups to liters	Cups by .236
Pints to liters	Pints by .473
Quarts to liters	Quarts by .946
Gallons to liters	Gallons by 3.785
Inches to centimeters	Inches by 2.54

Oven Temperatures

To convert Fahrenheit to Celsius, subtract 32 from Fahrenheit, multiply the result by 5, then divide by 9.

Description	Fahrenheit	Celsius	British Gas Mark
Very cool	200°	95°	0
Very cool	225°	110°	¼
Very cool	250°	120°	½
Cool	275°	135°	1
Cool	300°	150°	2
Warm	325°	165°	3
Moderate	350°	175°	4
Moderately hot	375°	190°	5
Fairly hot	400°	200°	6
Hot	425°	220°	7
Very hot	450°	230°	8
Very hot	475°	245°	9

Common Ingredients & Their Approximate Equivalents

1 cup uncooked white rice = 185 grams

1 cup all-purpose flour = 140 grams

1 stick butter
(4 ounces • ½ cup • 8 tablespoons) = 110 grams

1 cup butter
(8 ounces • 2 sticks • 16 tablespoons) = 220 grams

1 cup brown sugar, firmly packed = 225 grams

1 cup granulated sugar = 200 grams

Information compiled from a variety of sources, including *Recipes into Type* by Joan Whitman and Dolores Simon (Newton, MA: Biscuit Books, 1993); *The New Food Lover's Companion* by Sharon Tyler Herbst (Hauppauge, NY: Barron's, 2013); and *Rosemary Brown's Big Kitchen Instruction Book* (Kansas City, MO: Andrews McMeel, 1998).

LOCAL COLOR

Chapter 1

Pages xii-1

Central Grocery
923 Decatur Street
New Orleans, LA
504-523-1620
✦ Best muffuletta
 sandwiches in town.

Pages 3, 94, 100-101

Parkway Bakery and Tavern
538 Hagan Avenue
New Orleans, LA
504-482-3047
✦ Where we go for
 po'boys and more.

Pages 6, 140-141, 145, 147

Kenney's Seafood
400 Pontchartrain Drive
Slidell, LA
985-643-2717
✦ Go *See* my friend and
 favorite fishmonger,
 Brian Cappy.

Chapter 2

Pages 24-25

August
301 Tchoupitoulas Street
New Orleans, LA
504-299-9777
✦ Our flagship restaurant
 glows at night.

Chapter 5

Pages 80-81

Creole Tomato mural at AJ's Produce Co.
3162 Chartres Street
New Orleans, LA
✦ AJ's has supplied our
 area for over 30 years.

Pages 82-83, 114-115, 121

Camellia Produce
2810 William Tell Street
Slidell, LA
985-640-4297
✦ Tara and Jack Collier
 sell the freshest local
 produce around.

Pages 98-99

Blue Plate sign
1315 South Jefferson Davis Parkway
New Orleans, LA
✦ Still my favorite
 mayonnaise. Their old
 factory is now home to
 popular artist lofts.

Chapter 10

Pages 156-157

Cleaver & Co.
3917 Baronne Street
New Orleans, LA
504-277-3830
✦ These young guys run
 a great old-fashioned,
 locally sourced
 butcher shop.

Chapter 3

Pages 40-41

Zatarain's mural
On the side of the
Queen & Crescent Hotel
344 Camp Street
New Orleans, LA
✦ Love Zatarain's spice
blend seasonings,
mccormick.com.

Pages 46, 48-49, 182, 195

Lucullus
610 Chartres Street
New Orleans, LA
504-528-9620
✦ Right in the heart of
the Quarter, our stellar
source for culinary
antiques.

Pages 60-61

Pontalba Buildings
On North Peters and
St. Ann Streets at
Jackson Square
New Orleans, LA
✦ Many a celebration
happens on those
apartment balconies.

Chapter 4

Pages 76, 130-131

**Sidewalk art and mural
on old molasses depot,
Bywater**
3027 Chartres Street
New Orleans, LA
✦ Sidewalk outside and
mural opposite Dr. Bob's
funky folk art studio.

Chapter 11

Pages 166-167

Crystal Preserves sign
Off the Ponchartrain
Expressway overpass
at Carrollton and
Tulane Avenues
New Orleans, LA
✦ The sign for the iconic
hot sauce has been
restored. The factory
has moved.

Pages 174-175, 178-179

**Angelo Brocato
Italian Ice Cream &
Pastry**
214 North Carrollton
Avenue
New Orleans, LA
504-486-0078
✦ For over a hundred
years, Brocato's has
been the place for
Italian pastries.

Page 191

Le Croissant d'Or
617 Ursulines Avenue
New Orleans, LA
504-524-4663
✦ Beautiful little shop
for pastry and coffee
in the Quarter.

Page 199

**Leidenheimer's
Baking Co.**
1501 Simon Bolivar Avenue
New Orleans, LA
504-525-1575
✦ Since 1896, they've
made the French
bread for po'boys
sold throughout
New Orleans.

INDEX

Andrews McMeel Publishing
a division of Andrews McMeel Universal
1130 Walnut Street, Kansas City, Missouri 64106

www.andrewsmcmeel.com

www.chefjohnbesh.com

16 17 18 19 20 SDB 10 9 8 7 6 5 4 3

ISBN: 978-1-4494-6917-7

Library of Congress Control Number: 2015930418

PRODUCED AND EDITED BY Dorothy Kalins, Dorothy Kalins Ink, LLC
BOOK DESIGN: Don Morris, Don Morris Design
PHOTOGRAPHS: Maura McEvoy
ILLUSTRATIONS: Nick G. Botner

Andrews McMeel Publishing, LLC
EDITOR: Jean Z. Lucas
CREATIVE DIRECTOR: Tim Lynch
PRODUCTION EDITOR: Maureen Sullivan
PRODUCTION MANAGER: Carol Coe
DEMAND PLANNER: Sue Eikos